ESSENTIAL BOOK OF GEAR

A comprehensive guide to guit~
and effects for the de~

Alfred Music
P.O. Box 10003
Van Nuys, CA 91410-0003
alfred.com

Copyright © MMXIII by Alfred Music
All rights reserved. Printed in USA.

ISBN-10: 0-7390-9444-0 (Book & CD)
ISBN-13: 978-0-7390-9444-0 (Book & CD)

CD recorded in Baltimore, Maryland at Invisible Sound Studios and The Dojo

Cover photographs: Tobias Hurwitz

Equipment on cover: Mesa/Boogie Express 5:25 combo amp courtesy of Mesa Engineering
Boss MT-2 Metal Zone, DD-1 Digital Delay, TU-1 Chromatic Tuner, and CS-3 Compression Sustainer courtesy of Roland Corp.
The Rat courtesy of Pro Co Sound • Mini Q-Tron and Small Stone Phase Shifter courtesy of Electro-Harmonix • Philosopher's Tone courtesy of Pigtronix
Pedalboard courtesy of Furman • Axe-FX II courtesy of Fractal Audio Systems • Marshall JVM 100-watt half stack courtesy of Marshall Amplification
Vox wah-wah courtesy of Vox Amplification • Fender Deluxe combo amp, Fender Stratocaster, and Fender Telecaster courtesy of Fender Musical Instruments
Gibson ES-120 and Gibson SG Standard courtesy of Gibson USA

Alfred Cares. Contents printed on 100% recycled paper.

CONTENTS

ABOUT THE AUTHOR

GIT graduate Tobias Hurwitz resides in Baltimore, Maryland where he has been avidly playing rock guitar since 1977. In the summertime, Tobias directs the Rock Star Jam music camp in Baltimore and teaches at the Crown of the Continent Guitar Festival in Montana and the Ruby Mountain Guitar Summit in West Virginia. You can hear Tobias play his heart out on his three solo album releases—including *Zen Shred Zone,* which features cameos from technical guitar masters Michael Angelo Batio and Mattias Ai Eklundh, and, more recently, *Dreamer,* a collaboration with singer-songwriter extraordinaire Terry Gourley. Terry and Tobias perform regional gigs as a duo playing original music and classic covers. Tobias also offers guitar lessons in his home studio and over Skype.

Photo by J. Victor Elliot

Tobias has written 15 guitar books on a wide range of topics, from rock guitar and note-for-note transcriptions to zen guitar and how to get the best tones from your gear. He is widely published by major guitar magazines such as *Guitar Player* and was prominently featured in the best-selling book *Guitar Zero* by Gary Marcus. Tobias has over one million YouTube views and has jammed, recorded, and worked with a long list of world-renowned artists, including Dennis Chambers, Stanley Clarke, Victor Wooten, J. Geils, The Coasters, Philip Toshio Sudo, Bumblefoot, Paul Reed Smith, Sonia, Matt Halpern, and many more.

Tobias holds the patent and trademark to his innovative invention, The Shred-o-Meter, which is the world's first musical note speedometer, measuring the notes per second (NPS) that a guitarist can play. Tobias was named "Baltimore's Best Guitar Teacher" by the Baltimore *City Paper* and "Best Guitarist in the Mid-Atlantic" by *Music Monthly.*

Tobias endorses Paul Reed Smith Guitars, Ernie Ball Strings, Fractal Audio Systems, Pigtronix, and he is a M.A.C.E. Music recording artist in association with Michael Angelo Batio.

Visit www.tobiashurwitz.com to sign up for guitar lessons via Skype!

Acknowledgments

Special thanks to the light of my life, Terry Gourley, who is my longtime companion and has supported me throughout this project; and to the generous people who loaned me gear—Bill Gaphardt, Bill Hugo, Tim Lanocha, Zach Zeger, Billyjack Mast, and Christopher John Paul Murphy. Thanks to my friends in the Fractal Audio community—Matt Picone, Buddy Gill, and Dweezil Zappa. Thanks to Joe Berky of Sound Projects, Ron Cook of Bill's Music, and Zach Westphal of Guitar Center for answering a million questions. Thanks to Dave Nachodsky of Invisible Sound Studios/The American Tube Amp Museum. Thanks to Michael Angelo Batio for his help with photos and tones. Thanks to Alex White and Alex Cotsaris for help with photographs. Thanks to Burgess Speed for putting up with me!

INTRODUCTION

What electric guitarist isn't in love with the instrument itself and the gear that makes it sound so great? The first time I got close to an electric guitar was in my best friend Ric's workshop, where he had a makeshift guitar split in half on the workbench. Even though it was only hooked up to the 3" speaker of a transistor radio, when I hit the strings I was in heaven. Pretty soon, Ric and I were in a band together and I took the bus down to Bill's Music House in Catonsville, Maryland to get my first fuzz box. It was a Big Muff Pi. I'll never forget sitting around with my teenage friends just leaving the guitar leaning against a towering silver sparkle Custom amp and twisting the three knobs on that shiny Big Muff, filtering through luscious waves of thick static noise. But, to us, it wasn't just noise—it was music!

The passion didn't stop there. Like many of you, I explored guitars, pedals, processors, the Rockman X-100, and more! I even liked the smell of my new Whirlwind curly guitar cable. Soon, I was recording on a washing machine-sized 2" tape deck, cutting vinyl records, and then CDs. Not unpredictably, I lusted after Marshall amps and when I got one, I caught it on fire before learning how to hook up the speakers correctly! I was gigging for a living seven nights a week, learning to use complex computer programs, making a career of music, writing books and magazine articles about it, and all the while questing, yearning, and searching for and sometimes even achieving the perfect tone!

So, now I'm writing this book, and I must somehow decide what to include in the 128 pages of this manuscript. I could easily write a hundred pages on just my Paul Reed Smith Custom 24 and my Fractal Audio Systems Axe-FX II, but there is so much to say about not only my own sonic journey, but the evolution of the electric guitar and the countless devices that modify and enhance its tone as well.

This is certainly a huge topic that is deeply interwoven into many aspects of world economy and culture. We'll be getting into the history of it all, the major innovations that came along the way, the guitar itself, amps, the physics of sound, the sometimes cryptic terminology that manufacturers and techs use, tubes, noise, how to adjust a truss rod, signal flow, ohmage, epic signature artist tones, and much, much more. Read on and enjoy!

 **Track 00**   A compact disc is available with this book. Using the disc will help make learning more enjoyable and the information more meaningful. Much of the equipment covered in this book is demonstrated on the CD so that you are able to *hear* how it sounds in addition to reading about it. The symbol to the left, with the appropriate track number, appears next to each description of what is being demonstrated.

PART 1: THE HISTORY OF GUITAR GEAR

THE 1930s

Despite the stock market crash of 1929, which plunged America into the Great Depression, the 1930s were a time of significant technological innovation on multiple fronts. Along with the invention of frozen food, color film, the chocolate chip cookie, and a host of other conveniences, the electric guitar was born in 1931.

The First Electric Guitars

Jazz guitarists, such as Eddie Durham, Charlie Christian, Les Paul, and George Barnes, as well as Hawaiian slide players, needed to be louder to cut through the band. Many had tinkered with various methods of attaching microphones to banjos, violins, acoustic guitars, and other instruments, but it seems the "Frying Pan Guitar," invented by George Beauchamp, claims the distinction of being the first truly electric guitar. Beauchamp had also helped to develop the Dobro Resonator Guitar and co-founded the National String Instrument Corporation, through which he was acquainted with Rickenbacker, who would soon be manufacturing the first mass-produced electric guitars. The Hawaiian lap steel guitar pictured below (officially the model A-22 manufactured by Rickenbacker Electro Instruments) was the first electric guitar and earned its nickname due to its obvious resemblance to a frying pan.

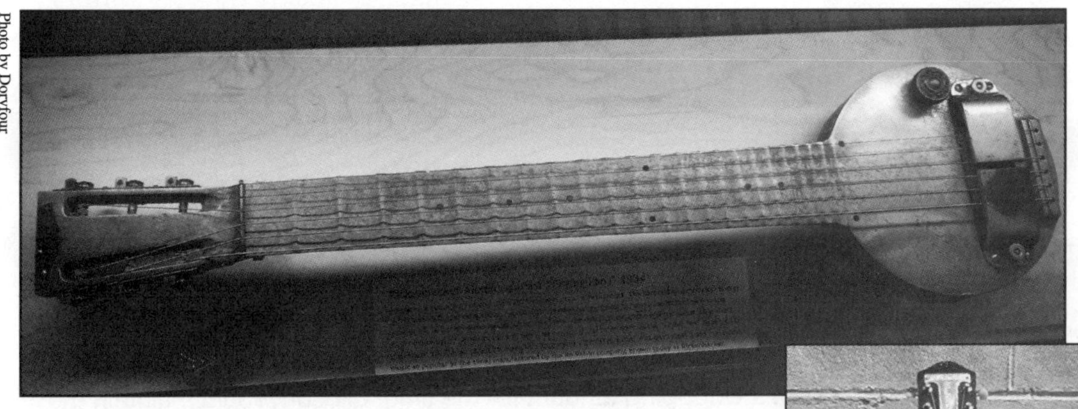

Photo by Doryfour

"The Frying Pan." Note the two large magnets that acted as pickups on this aluminum-bodied guitar.

The ripples of this important invention would be felt around the world, particularly in country music, which is now difficult to imagine without the inclusion of electric slide guitar in its many forms, be it the lap steel, pedal steel, or bottleneck slide. Close on the heels of the A-22 came the Electro Spanish Guitar, also by Rickenbacker, pictured to the right.

Photo Courtesy of Eben Cole/Cole Music Company

The Electro Spanish Guitar.

The first documented electric guitar performance was on an Electro Spanish Guitar played by Gage Brewer in Wichita, Kansas on Halloween of 1932. The instrument featured steel strings for magnetic response, a traditional Spanish headstock, F-holes, and a trapeze tailpiece, but no volume or tone controls. The headstocks on the earliest models simply said "Electro" before they were re-labeled as "Rickenbacker."

Beauchamp was not awarded a patent for the invention of the A-22 until 1937, which allowed other manufacturers to simultaneously produce electric guitars, such as the Gibson ES-150 and the Epiphone Electar, which were both marketed in 1936. Many other companies introduced electric models before 1937, including Audio-Vox, Volu-Tone, and Vega.

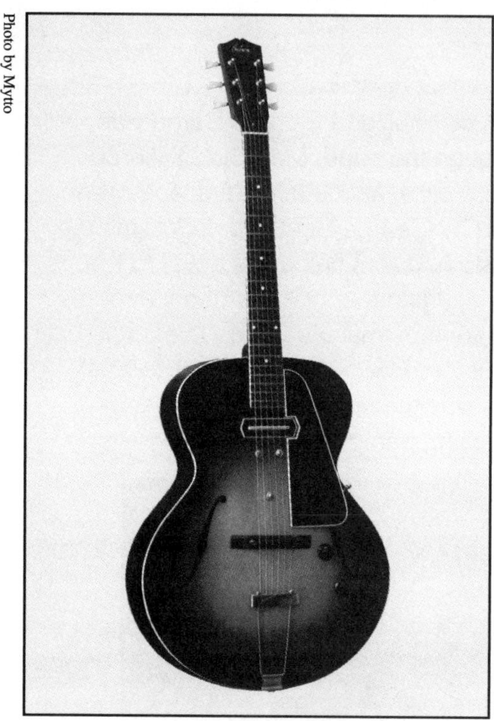

The Gibson ES-150.

The ES in "Gibson ES-150" stood for Electro Spanish, and the model number 150 indicated the price point, which was $150, a whopping amount for the time. Gibson would maintain the price point in the model number for some time, most famously with the Gibson Super-400, which retailed for $400.

The First Amplifiers

In addition to his electric guitar innovation, George Beauchamp had included primitive drawings for a guitar amplifier in his 1932 patent designs for the "Frying Pan."

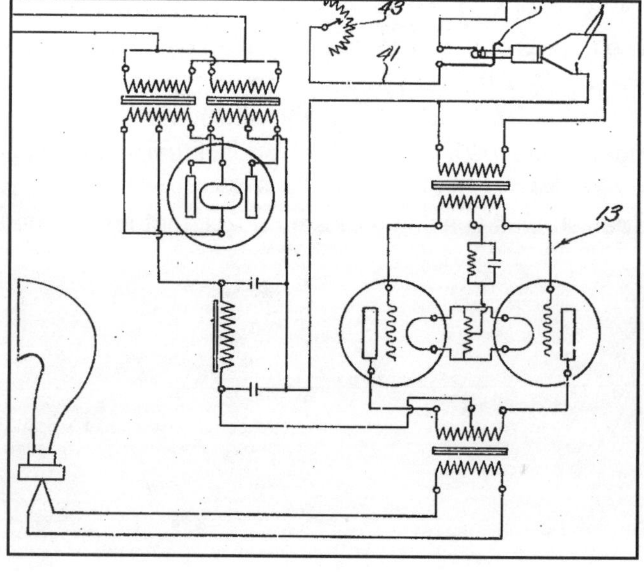

Beauchamp's 1932 amp schematic.

Beauchamp's drawings led to the earliest production-line guitar amps: the Rickenbacker M Series (but before the M Series came a few prototypes simply called "The Speaker"). This early tube amplifier appeared in the Rickenbacker catalog and was pictured with the Frying Pan Guitar. Gibson also produced amplifiers in the 1930s, among them was the EH-100, which was sold as a companion to their lap steel guitars.

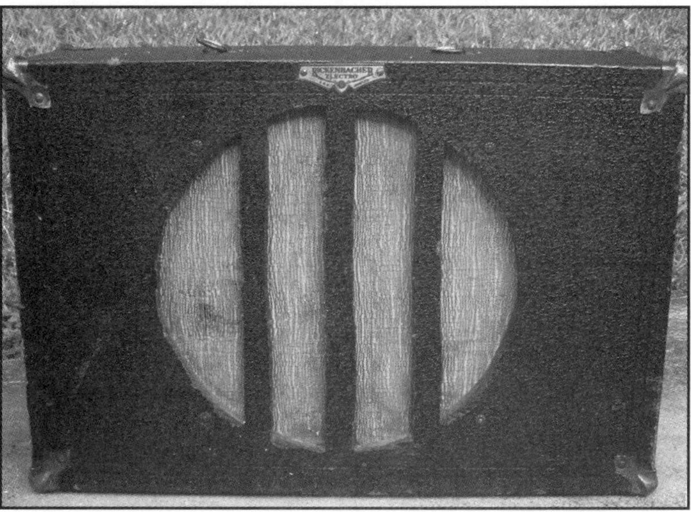
Early Rickenbacker prototype amp, known as "The Speaker."

Soon, the M Series would take over and eventually inspire Leo Fender to build a whole new breed of amplifiers in the 1940s.

1930s Rickenbacker M Series Tube Amplifier.

Early 7-String Guitar

In 1938, jazz guitar pioneer George Van Eps began playing 7-string guitars to better incorporate bass lines into his chord-melody playing. He acquired a custom-built Epiphone 7-string guitar and was able to work in chords, melody, and walking bass lines thanks to the lower 7th string. His playing inspired a number of modern jazz players—like Bucky Pizzarelli, John Pizzarelli, and Lenny Breau—to use 7-string guitars.

John Pizzarelli at the 2001 Umbria Jazz Festival in Perugia, Italy.

Early Talk Box

Amazingly, 1970s-style talk box technology was experimented with in 1939 by steel guitarist Alvino Rey. The device he used was called a Sonavox, which was operated on a microphone strapped to the performer's neck. Rey scored several "talking steel" hits with the device in the early '40s, but the technology disappeared until roughly 1969 when it was revisited by the Kustom Company.

THE 1940s

The recovery from the Great Depression, partly due to President Franklin D. Roosevelt's New Deal program and the World War II jobs boom, started a long, upward trend in America's economy. This occurred roughly from 1940 to 1970 and was a fertile period for musical instrument innovation as well as general technological advancement. The '40s saw the invention of the atomic bomb, the electronic digital computer, the microwave oven, and many other modern wonders, including the solid-body electric guitar! Swing was the most popular music of the day, and it was played everywhere—from Harlem's Apollo Theater to the smokiest clubs of Paris, where the likes of Django Reinhardt played on, even in the face of Nazi occupation.

"The Log" by Les Paul

By the mid-1930s, Les Paul had established himself as a jazz guitarist on the cutting edge of technology by playing electric guitar live on the radio and tinkering with guitar pickups and recording methods. In 1941, he presented "The Log" to the Epiphone factory for consideration. The Log was an early solid-body electric guitar prototype with removable sides. This allowed Paul to demonstrate that the body of the guitar was not really necessary for producing an amplified sound. At first, he would play the guitar with the sides attached and then he'd remove them. To the amazement of the audience, the sound stayed the same.

Les Paul's "The Log" resides in the Country Music Hall of Fame.

The Myth of the First Electric Guitar

In popular mythology, Les Paul is known as the inventor of the solid-body electric guitar, but this isn't really the case. At the time The Log was built, the Vivi-Tone company already offered a full line of solid-body electric guitars. As a player with his finger on the pulse of modern technology, it's hard to believe Les was unaware of these guitars. Regardless of its position in the historical lineage of the solid-body guitar, The Log was still the main guitar Les Paul used from 1941–1949. He played it on the road with The Andrews Sisters, on his many radio hits from that period, and with Bing Crosby. It is clearly an example of a very early and truly iconic solid-body electric guitar! The solid-body electric guitar wouldn't fully emerge until the 1950s.

Leslie Rotating Speaker

1941 was the year signal processing was born, in the form of the Leslie Rotating Speaker. It was designed by Don Leslie in an attempt to improve the sound of the Hammond organ. He originally called it the Vibratone, and the speaker was also known by several other names, including Brittain Speakers, Hollywood Speakers, and Crawford Speakers, before returning to the name Leslie Vibratone in 1946. It was the first mechanical chorusing device and operated on the *Doppler Effect,* which was discovered by the Austrian physicist Christian Doppler in 1842. The Doppler Effect causes a change in frequency generated by a moving sound source. As the source approaches the listener, the waves bunch together, raising the pitch. When the source is aligned with the listener, the waves are unaffected and when the source moves away, the pitches are lowered. All the while, the original sound can also be heard. This oscillation of pitch mixed into the original sound has come to be called *chorusing*.

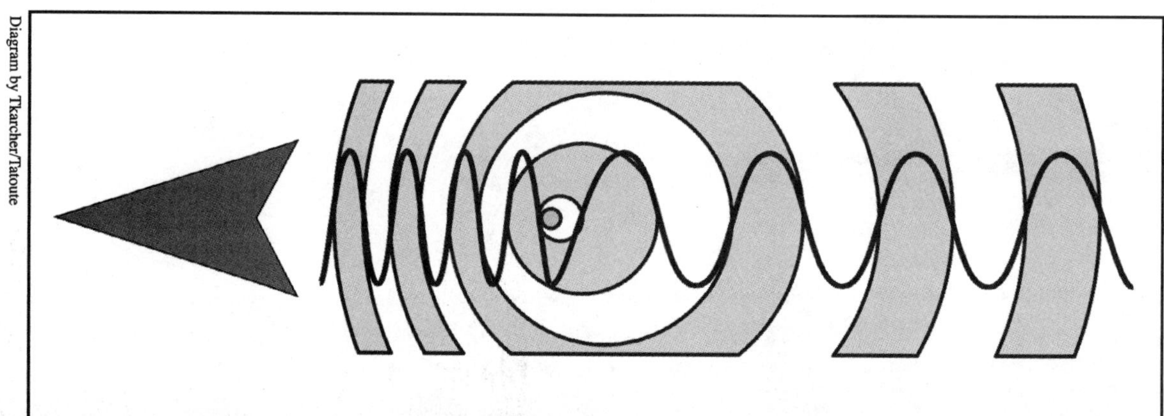

Visual representation of the Doppler Effect.

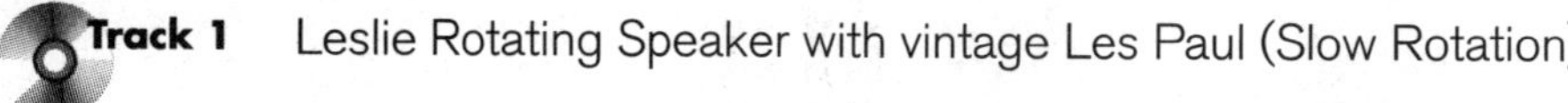
Track 1   Leslie Rotating Speaker with vintage Les Paul (Slow Rotation)

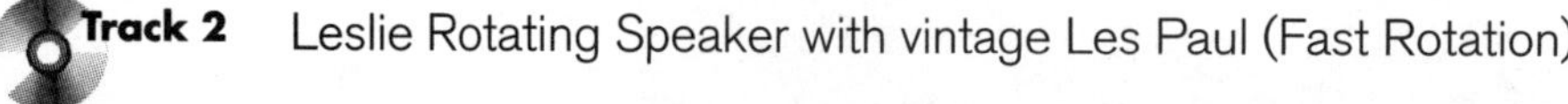
Track 2   Leslie Rotating Speaker with vintage Les Paul (Fast Rotation)

In the '40s, the Leslie Rotating Speaker was mostly used for keyboard instruments, but, later, guitarists such as George Harrison, Stevie Ray Vaughan, Peter Frampton, and Jerry Garcia began setting themselves apart from everyone else by using it for both rhythm and lead work.

Flanging

The next innovation would come from Les Paul. In a stroke of genius, he invented *flanging* in the early 1940s and first recorded the new sound in 1945 on "Mamie's Boogie." He achieved a new effect by syncing two reel-to-reel tape machines and slightly changing the speed of one of them with a *Variac*. This created a slight delay between the two signals, something below 20 milliseconds, that caused the sweeping sound known as *flanging*. The Variac is a device that features a dial used to gradually lower or raise the voltage it supplies. Paul cycled the voltage down and up to vary the speed of one of the machines. Others simply laid a finger lightly on the rim of the tape reel, or flange, as it is called, to control the speed by hand.

Leo Fender

Leo Fender, born in Anaheim, California in 1909, eventually became a self-employed radio repairman in 1938. He met Clayton (Doc) Kauffman and the two started K&F Manufacturing Corporation in 1945. They made amps and electric lap steel guitars, but very few of their products have survived. Kauffman left the company in February 1946, and it become known as the Fender Electric Instrument Manufacturing Company, or just "Fender" for short. Fender continued to manufacture amplifiers and electric lap steel guitars in California.

The first Fender amplifier was the wood-housed Model 26 made in 1946. The Princeton amp arrived in 1947, and the distinctive look of tweed-covered amps was introduced with the Champ in 1948.

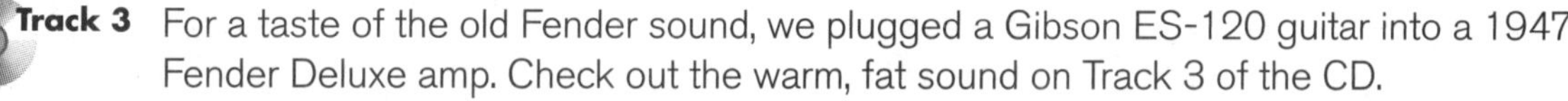

Track 3   For a taste of the old Fender sound, we plugged a Gibson ES-120 guitar into a 1947 Fender Deluxe amp. Check out the warm, fat sound on Track 3 of the CD.

Photo by Quinn A. Burson

1946 Fender Model 26.

Photo by BrotherAbel

1953 Fender Champ.

The Transistor

In 1948, Bell Laboratories physicists William Shockley, Walter Brattain, and John Bardeen invented the transistor, a semiconductor device used to amplify and switch electronic signals and electrical power.

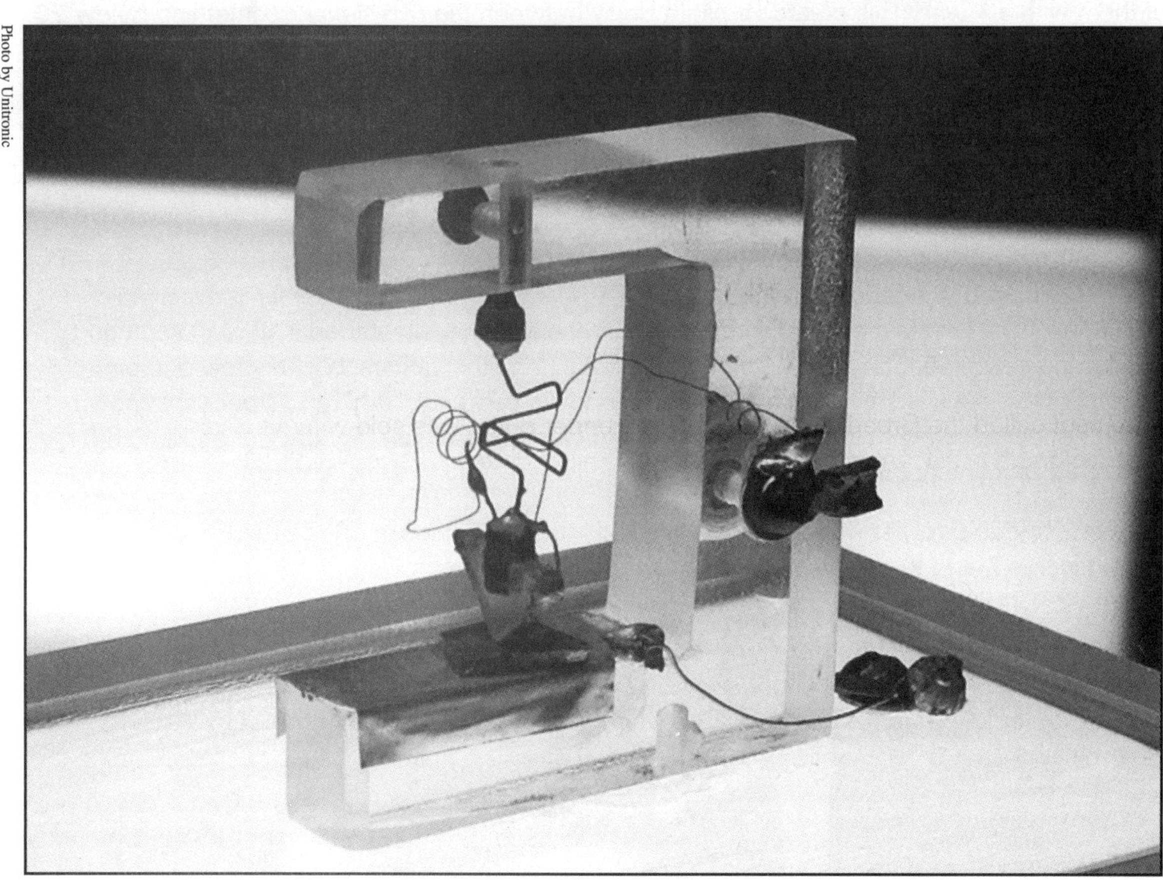

The first transistor—invented by Shockley, Brattain, and Bardeen—is on display at Bell Laboratories.

The small, lightweight, and reliable transistor became a suitable replacement for the vacuum tube and paved the way for the age of modern electronics. Transistor technology went on to create countless pieces of guitar gear and various other electronic gadgets.

THE 1950s

By the 1950s, World War II had ended and the Cold War was heating up. Nuclear bomb testing was on the rise, the space race was beginning, and a strong anti-communist sentiment was building in America. Television had been invented as well as the plastic Coca-Cola bottle and paper copying. The music scene was diversifying and growing to include various genres, such as jazz, folk, blues, skiffle, the new sounds of doo-wop, and rockabilly. Crooners like Frank Sinatra and Tony Bennett charmed the masses, but something even bigger was breaking. Little Richard, Chuck Berry, Elvis Presley, Bill Haley, and others were laying the groundwork for the biggest music craze ever: rock and roll!

Fender Broadcaster

In the autumn of 1950, the first mass-produced solid-body electric guitar was released by Fender. It was called the Broadcaster and was essentially what we know now as a Telecaster; the name was quickly changed to Telecaster due to a request from Gretsch who had released a drumset called the Broadkaster earlier. The Fender guitar was sold without a name for a short while before the Telecaster logo was used on the headstock.

1950 Fender Broadcaster.

The Broadcaster was easy to transport and maintain with its slim design, bolt-on neck, and easy-access panel for working on electronics. At that time, the electronics of a guitar were typically accessed through the sound holes, which was a much more awkward method. The neck on the Broadcaster was made from a single piece of maple without a separate glued-on fretboard, which was typical at the time. The body was made of either ash or alder wood. The guitar delivered a clear, bright sound with several tone options due to its two pickups and three-position blade switch. The adjustable truss rod and bridge assisted with achieving good intonation and playability, and the guitar could reach high stage volumes without any of the feedback problems associated with hollow-body guitars. This major milestone of innovation with the Broadcaster left an indelible mark on guitar design and helped to usher in a bold new era of solid-body electric guitars.

Fender Precision Bass

In 1951, Fender delivered another classic with the Precision Bass (also known as the P-Bass), a solid-body electric bass companion to their solid-body electric guitar, which by then was called the Telecaster.

1956 Fender Precision Bass.

Gibson Les Paul

In 1951, the Gibson company became aware of Fender's successes with solid-body electric instrument sales and decided it was time to really explore Les Paul's idea with The Log. Gibson's president Ted McCarty brought Les Paul to the company as a consultant and by 1952 the Gibson Les Paul guitar was on the market. McCarty actually had more to do with designing the iconic guitar than Les Paul, but it was certainly a collaboration.

Photo courtesy of Detlef Alder, www.guitarpoint.de

1952 Les Paul.

The Gibson Les Paul featured a radically different design from the Fender Telecaster and became Gibson's flagship model. Its carved gold top exuded an elegant yet traditional appearance. The neck was attached to the body by a dovetail joint instead of bolted on, and the headstock was angled back instead of straight. These last two features improved the sustain and stability of the instrument. The Les Paul guitar featured single-coil P-90 pickups, a trapeze tailpiece, a Brazilian rosewood fingerboard, and a carved maple top over the mahogany body. The slightly shorter scale length of the neck (24.75" vs. 25.5" on Fender) and the bulkier wood of the body gave the Les Paul a fatter and more aggressive sound than the Telecaster.

The electronics were quite remarkable, too, featuring a three-position toggle switch which allowed for the selection of either of the two pickups separately or a combination of both. Since each P-90 pickup had its own volume and tone controls, it was easy to switch from a warm, low-volume sound to a brighter, louder sound just by flicking the toggle switch.

Gibson and Fender competed for market share by releasing iconic instruments such as the whammy bar-equipped Fender Stratocaster in 1954 and the double cutaway Gibson SG in 1961.

Track 4   On track 4 of the CD, we plugged a vintage Telecaster into a 1957 Fender Deluxe and dialed in a '50s rock and roll tone. Enjoy!

Tremolo and Vibrato

The terms *tremolo* and *vibrato* can be a little confusing because both have been used to describe the pitch-changing action of the whammy bar on a Fender Stratocaster, but tremolo and vibrato are actually quite different effects. Tremolo is a cyclical variation of volume, and vibrato is a cyclical variation of pitch. Amplifiers that offered these as built-in features were available in the 1940s, but Fender began marketing the first tremolo- and vibrato-equipped amps in the mid-1950s. In 1955, Fender introduced the Tremolux, which was quickly followed by the Vibrolux in 1956. To hear the difference between vibrato and tremolo, check out the next two CD tracks.

 **Track 5**   Vintage Magnatone Vibrato

 **Track 6**   Vintage Vox Tremolo

The Origins of Fuzz

The first fuzz tones were attained by playing through damaged equipment, sometimes unintentionally and sometimes by design. Nashville's legendary Quonset Hut Studio, built in 1951, was an early arena for fuzz evolution. When the studio console malfunctioned, producing a fuzzy tone on one channel, the engineers and players decided to keep certain fuzzy tracks because they liked the sound. After the console was repaired, requests for that exciting, modern sound came pouring in, and the search for fuzz was on! In 1956, guitarist Paul Burlison of The Rock and Roll Trio achieved an influential fuzz tone by intentionally dislodging one of his amp's tubes before recording "The Train Kept A-Rollin'." Burlison learned the trick by accidentally dropping his amp at a Philadelphia gig, which resulted in a fuzzy sound that he loved and kept using. Burlison's recording of "The Train Kept A-Rollin'" turned out to be very influential and important to the popularity of fuzz. In 1958, Link Wray punched holes in the speakers of his Premier amp with a pen to get a fuzz sound for the power chords in his song "Rumble." At around the same time, blues guitarist Roy Buchanan sliced the speakers in his Fender Vibrolux amp while chasing the same coveted sound. Apparently, the destruction of costly equipment was no obstacle when it came to getting the highly desired fuzz tone.

Quonset Hut Studio console, now residing in the Country Music Hall of Fame.

Tape Echo

The 1950s saw the rise of *tape echo* as a musical effect. At that time, reel-to-reel tape recorders were the norm and tape echo was achieved by varying the tape speed or the distance between the heads. The number of repeats was also variable with a feedback control. On the Echoplex pictured below, this control is labeled "Echo Repeats."

These tape echo concepts weren't exactly new, since Les Paul had been tinkering with them since 1934 when the only recording devices available were disc-cutting machines. German engineers had developed reel-to-reel machines in the '30s, but they were basically unheard of in America. By the '50s, Paul had gotten the notion that he would like to be able to hear previously recorded tracks while recording new ones in perfect sync. He ordered a custom-built Ampex 8-track tape recorder, which was likely the first muti-track recording deck. Therefore, Les Paul is credited with the invention of multi-track recording.

The Echosonic, designed by Ray Butts, was an early guitar amp that featured a built-in tape echo device. This innovative gadget was quickly adopted by players like Scotty Moore (Elvis's guitarist), Chet Atkins, and Carl Perkins. The short "slapback" effect produced by the Echosonic became a staple of early rock and roll, and rockabilly guitar tone. The Echosonic was a predecessor to the famed Echoplex device, made by Mike Battle in 1959, which is widely considered the gold standard of vintage tape echoes.

The Echoplex.

The Echosonic amp.

Other companies marketed tape echo devices at around the same time, including the EchoFonic by Fender. Over the next few decades, echo technology continued to march ahead in the forms of analog delay and then digital delay. Echo effects would soon be leveraged in countless directions to become an indispensable cornerstone of modern guitar effects.

Gibson Flying V

Another electric guitar evolution began to develop in the late 1950s. In 1959, Gibson introduced the "Flying V" body style, which was not only different in appearance, but was made from an unusual wood: korina.

1959 Gibson Flying V.

The V introduced the notion that a rock and roll electric guitar not only could, but probably should, look futuristic and unconventional. Guitar makers like B.C. Rich, Hamer, Steinberger, Dean, and Parker would all follow Gibson's lead by developing electric guitars with new and unique body shapes.

THE 1960s

The 1960s was a period of significant cultural and technological evolution both in the United States and abroad. The Beatles formed in Liverpool, England in 1960, influencing the world of music forever, and played their last public show in Manhattan in 1969—which was the same year the United States put a man on the moon and President Richard Nixon brought back the draft lottery. In 1964, Pete Townshend began smashing instruments on stage. The burgeoning hippie movement peaked at Haight-Ashbury in San Francisco in 1967 with the notorious "summer of love" and had its last glorious hurrah in 1969 at the Woodstock music festival where Jimi Hendrix gave "The Star Spangled Banner" a new voice and permanently carved the sound of Marshall amplification and whammy bar dives into the collective subconscious of mankind.

The quest for fuzz guitar tones and echoes that began in the 1950s was fully realized in the '60s. The exploratory psychedelic music movement, which included artists as diverse as The Beatles, Pink Floyd, The Grateful Dead, Jimi Hendrix, The Rolling Stones, and many others, fit hand in glove with the sonic innovations of companies like Vox, Electro-Harmonix, Marshall, and Maestro. A slew of new devices hit the market and were immediately consumed, spurring a craze in manufacturing innovation that lasted for decades.

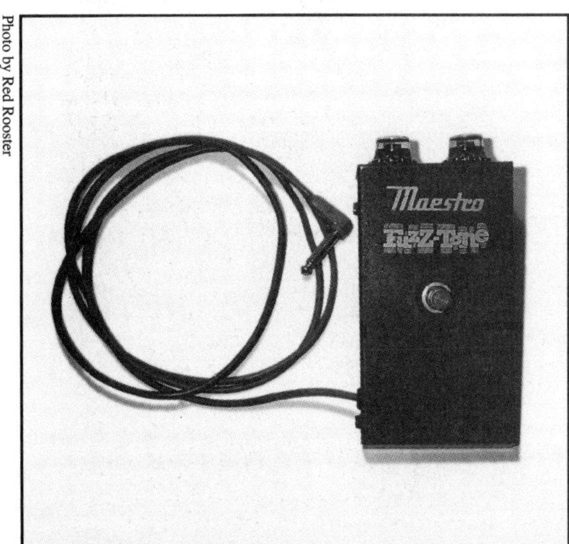

Early Maestro Fuzz Box.

Fuzz Boxes

The fuzz tones that had been so elusive in the '50s were made easily available by companies like Maestro, with its FZ-1 Fuzz Tone pedal, which was released in 1963 and took off in 1965 when Keith Richards used one to blast out the riff to "Satisfaction."

Roger Mayer built custom fuzz boxes for clients like Jimmy Page in the early '60s, and, by 1966, Jimi Hendrix was using the newly invented germanium transistor driven Fuzz Face and Octavia pedals, which can be heard on "Purple Haze." The germanium transistors sounded better than the silicon ones that were used in later models. Sola/Colorsound, Arbiter, Sam Ash, Vox, Mosrite, and others added their fuzzes to the fray and the game was on!

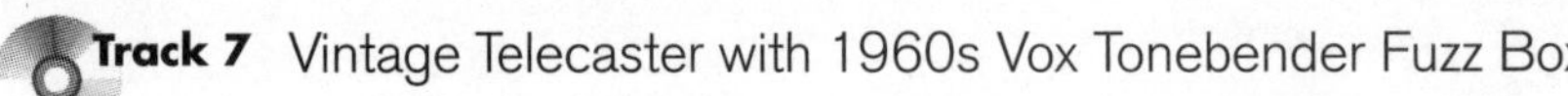

Track 7 Vintage Telecaster with 1960s Vox Tonebender Fuzz Box

Ring Modulation

Tom Oberheim, who worked for Maestro, developed the pre-existing technology of *ring modulation* into a guitar pedal form. Ring modulation was a key component of modular synthesizers such as the Moog synthesizer. Oberheim experimented with ring modulation in the context of film scoring for *The Planet of the Apes* and eventually Maestro would release the earliest ring modulator pedals. The ring modulator circuit eliminates the original signal and generates "side bands" of random sounding harmonics that are above and below the original. Depending on the usage, it can be extremely dissonant or somewhat melodic. An example of the haunting sound can be heard on the theme song for the 1960s sci-fi show *Dr. Who*.

Marshall Amps

Jim Marshall owned a small music shop in London where the likes of Pete Townshend and Ritchie Blackmore passed through asking for louder amps that could meet their needs on the big stage. So in 1962 Marshall unveiled the JTM 45, which was designed to compete with the pricey Fender amps that were being imported from America at the time. The JTM 45 featured 6L6 power tubes instead of the EL34s that would soon come to define the British sound.

Marshall JTM 45.

Marshall JTM 45: Beginning of the Marshall Stack

The JTM 45 was obviously influenced by Fender amps like the Bassman and Showman, both of which also featured 6L6 tubes, four jumpable inputs, and separate amp heads and speaker cabinets. The early Marshall 4x12" speaker cabinets were loaded with 15-watt Celestion speakers which sounded rougher and moved the amp in a new direction that was quickly appreciated by English rockers.

By 1965, Marshall had switched to EL34 power tubes which distorted more easily than 6L6s, and the JTM 45 began to evolve in step with the demands of rock musicians who sought out heavier sounds. Marshall unveiled 100-watt heads, stackable cabs, combos, and various other offerings as demand increased worldwide. Soon, the white plastic script logo was adopted and the now iconic look was complete. The increased wattage was finally satisfactory and the new impedance selector enabled the connection of two 4x12" cabs for users like Jimi Hendrix, who began chaining together the new Super Lead model 100-watt heads with stacked cabinets to create walls of Marshalls. Pete Townshend ended up switching to the brutally loud British made Hiwatt Amps, which he stayed with for the bulk of his career.

Swedish press image, original photographer unknown

Jimi Hendrix onstage in Sweden, 1967.

Track 8   Vintage Strat – '60s Fuzz Face – 1967 Marshall JTM 45 (Hendrix-style clean)

Track 9   Vintage Strat – '60s Fuzz Face – 1967 Marshall JTM 45 (Hendrix-style grit)

Track 10   Vintage Strat – '60s Fuzz Face – Vox wah – 1967 Marshall JTM 45 (Full-on Hendrix style)

Compression

In 1963, The Beatles were recording *Please Please Me* at London's Abbey Road Studios. The studio had a few external units that boosted frequencies or acted as equalizers, such as an EMI RS-127 presence booster that provided a 10db boost or cut at three fixed frequencies, but they had to build their own compressor/limiter. In those days, compression was only available as a custom-made studio processor. The processor at Abbey Road was called the TD114 and was used for Beatles recordings up through *A Hard Day's Night* in 1964. Later that year, when *Beatles for Sale* was being recorded, the studio began using the now-legendary Fairchild 660 limiter. In addition to the usual function of controlling dynamic levels, the Fairfield added presence and punch to any guitar or vocal passing through it, creating an easily noticeable improvement. (See page 27 for more on compressors.)

The "jangle" on Track 11 is reminiscent of The Beatles' 1960s sounds.

Track 11   1961 Les Paul with a 1963 Vox AC-30 2x12" combo

Fender in the 1960s

Fender was also active and influential in the 1960s. They set the standard for guitar reverb with their stand-alone 6G15 reverb unit, released in 1962. In 1964, the esteemed Fender Twin Reverb amp hit the market and remains to this day one of the greatest amps of all time.

CBS bought Fender in 1965, and, by 1966, changes were made to the product line that were eventually frowned upon by collectors of vintage gear. The term "Pre-CBS" refers to the most desirable Fender gear, all of which was made before 1966. This is not to say post-CBS Fender equipment is not worth collecting. For instance, a 1974 Stratocaster with a three-bolt neck in decent shape, depending on the model, can go for up to ten thousand dollars on today's market. Nonetheless, changes such as the use of cheaper plastics, the switch to Indian rosewood instead of the magical Brazilian rosewood for some of the fretboards, polyurethane finish instead of the original nitrocellulose lacquer, larger headstocks, and many other small modifications rendered the newer instruments less desirable. Nonetheless, Fender was still very much in the game and continued to offer innovative and popular products. In 1967, they released the Echo-Reverb unit and the Vibratone rotating speaker that was later used by Stevie Ray Vaughan on "Cold Shot."

Photo by Jurch

Fender Vibratone.

Acoustic note: *The Kaman company founded Ovation Instruments in 1965 with the goal of improving the sound of the acoustic guitar. In 1966, their research and development team determined that a semi-parabolic shape for the back would yield improved tone and the roundback acoustic guitar was born. The rounded back was made from Lyrachord, their patented material made up of interwoven layers of glass filament and bonding resin. It was also the first acoustic-electric guitar. Ovation continued to innovate new technologies in the coming decades.*

The Wah-Wah

The story of the wah-wah began in 1961 when Ampeg started experimenting with passive wah circuitry. This didn't actually lead very far, but engineer Brad Plunkett created an active bandpass filter with variable resonant frequency in 1966, and in 1967 Vox marketed the first active wah, the Clyde McCoy Wah-Wah, which was a potentiometer-based pedal much like the Cry Baby wah we are familiar with today. Named after the famous saxophonist, it was intended to emulate muted horn sounds. The foot pedal swept through a range of frequencies, accentuating higher ones when it was rocked toward the toe position. Think "Voodoo Chile (Slight Return)" by Hendrix or the theme song from *Shaft* for the classic wah-wah sound. By 1968, wahs were in common usage and, in the '70s, they had taken hold as an indispensable tool for professional and aspiring guitarists—which is still the case today.

Photo by Marco Raaphorst

Vox wah-wah pedal.

Innovations in the Late 1960s

The late '60s featured so many exciting events that it's hard to decide what to include. In 1965, Hartley Peavey founded Peavey Electronics in the United States. Over the coming decades, Peavey made many significant contributions to the industry, particularly in guitar design. Sola Colorsound started in London in 1965 with a line of visually stimulating pedals that livened up many rigs for the next decade or two. The now-legendary Kustom amp line, featuring solid-state technology, was launched in 1967.

The premier issue of *Guitar Player* magazine hit the streets in 1967. It was the very first American magazine dedicated to guitar and immediately began to influence both guitar players and the gear they used.

In 1968, Jon Nady developed the first wireless guitar system, and at around the same time Randall Smith modified Fender Princeton amps for more power and preamp tube distortion. Later, these would be known as Mesa/Boogie amps.

Electro-Harmonix was founded in 1968 by Mike Matthews and started their accessory line with the LPB-1 (Linear Power Booster). This little gadget offered a clean boost strong enough to overdrive any tube amp or to simply provide a louder sound for lead work; the LPB-1 is still popular today.

In 1969, Tychobrahe was founded and released their own version of the Octavia pedal. Univox introduced the Uni-Vibe pedal, which was used by Hendrix on "Little Wing," "The Wind Cries Mary," and "Voodoo Chile (Slight Return)." And, as a punctuation mark to the decade, Led Zeppelin released their groundbreaking debut in 1969!

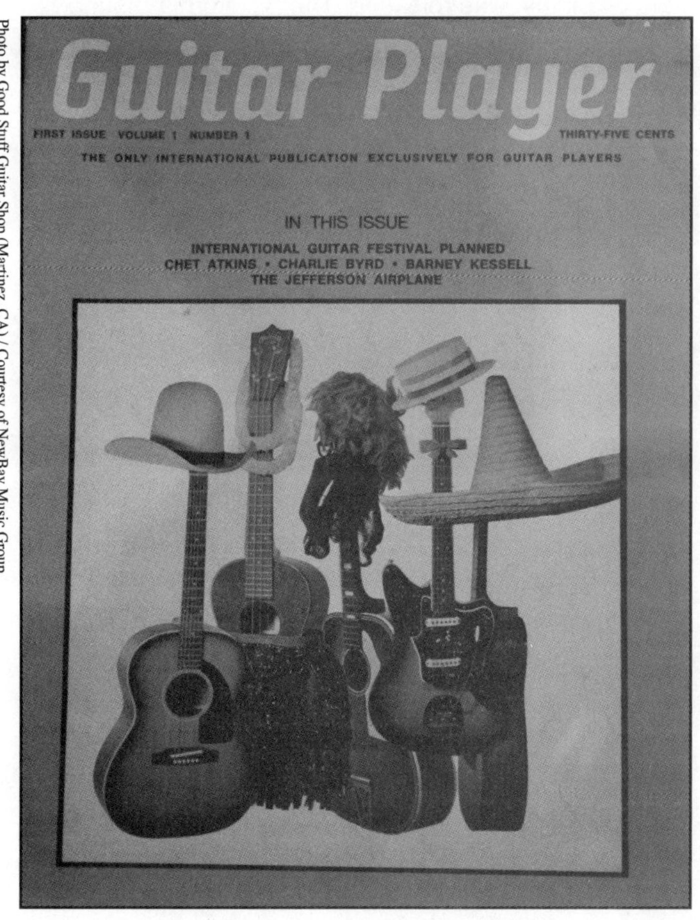

First issue of *Guitar Player* magazine.

THE 1970s

The 1970s saw the demise of the hippie movement, the rise of environmentalism, the end of the Vietnam War, and several economic crises, including the OPEC oil embargo of 1973. Muscle cars equipped with 8-track players thundered down rural roads blasting music that would soon be called "classic rock" while Skylab, NASA's first space station, orbited above. The microchip was invented and new musical styles emerged, including disco, punk rock, and heavy metal, the latter by way of the release of Black Sabbath's self-titled debut in 1970. The jazz fusion movement, sparked by Miles Davis's album *Bitches Brew* (1970), also flourished during this period. This was the decade in which the explosion of gear ideas that had been building since the '40s finally peaked, a time when the bulk of all the effects guitarists now enjoy became readily available—at least in their original forms.

Mesa/Boogie

The amp maker Mesa/Boogie was founded in 1970 by Randall Smith, and the company released its first official product, the Mark I, in 1971. Early endorser Carlos Santana had a bit to do with naming the brand by exclaiming that the amp really "boogied" while testing an early prototype, which was basically a modified Fender Princeton. The Mark I was a different breed of amp, and it quickly became known as a superior product. It was the first guitar amp to feature an extra preamp tube and several gain stages. In short, Smith had invented the first high-gain amp, and things would never be the same!

The unique wicker grill and polished hardwood enclosure gave the Boogie an outstanding appearance and hinted at the high quality within. Graphic EQ and reverb were soon added, and by 1978 the Mark II, with two foot switchable channels, was released. The "California" sound of cascading gain stages with 12AX7 preamp tubes and 6L6 power tubes, which became synonymous with Mesa/Boogie, was a significant advancement in amplifier design. The sound was soon adopted by Carlos Santana and a virtual "who's who" of guitar heroes worldwide.

Early 1980s Mesa/Boogie Mark II.

Talk Box

The 1970s also marked the era of the *talk box.* The Kustom "Bag," which became available in 1969, was the first talk box and its funky vibe is perhaps unsurpassed in the world of guitar effects. It was a truly ingenious device that allowed a guitarist to "speak" with his guitar in a mechanical but melodic voice.

The Bag held a small speaker enclosure whose output was fed into a short length of thin blue plastic tubing that was held in the performer's mouth. The Bag was connected between the amp and speaker cabinet with an included 20 ft. "Y" cable with male and female ends, so, when activated, the signal was diverted to the bag's driver. The sound stopped coming out of the amp, when The Bag was activated, and was fed into the guitarist's mouth through the tubing. As the player silently mouthed out the words, the resulting sound was picked up by a vocal microphone and amplified through the P.A. system. Jeff Beck and Stevie Wonder both used The Bag.

In 1972, Bob Heil produced a more powerful and reliable floor pedal called Talk Box that represented the state of the art of the day. The Talk Box was most famously used by Peter Frampton in songs like "Show Me the Way" and "Do You Feel Like I Do." It had a much more powerful speaker than The Bag and featured thicker tubing, but the basic idea was the same. Joe Walsh's *Rocky Mountain Way* and Chaka Kahn's *Tell Me Something Good* were also examples of 1970s talk box hits.

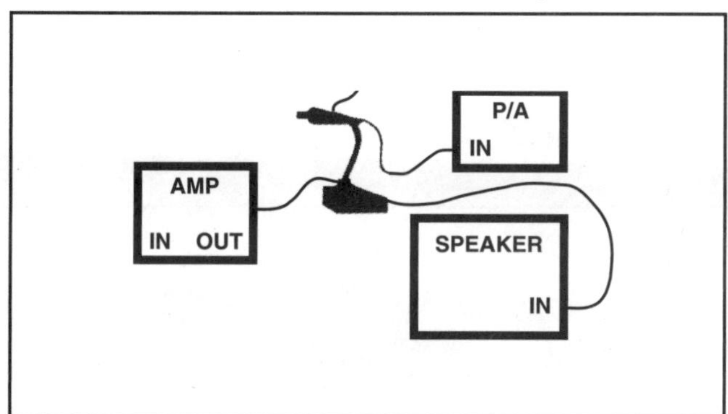

Talk box configuration.

Talk box used by Peter Frampton on the iconic 1970s album *Frampton Comes Alive.*

Phase Shifter

The *phase shifter,* which had begun to emerge in the late 1960s amid attempts at rotating speaker simulation, really took hold in the early '70s. In 1971, the Maestro PS-1 phase shifter was introduced. The phasing process splits the audio signal and sweeps one half with a narrow bandwidth filter. This notch creates an ever-changing spectrum of phase cancellations when combined with the dry signal. The sweeping sound that results is similar to flanging and chorusing but has its own unique timbre. The controls generally include three knobs: rate, depth, and resonance. These control the speed, depth, and intensity of the effect, respectively.

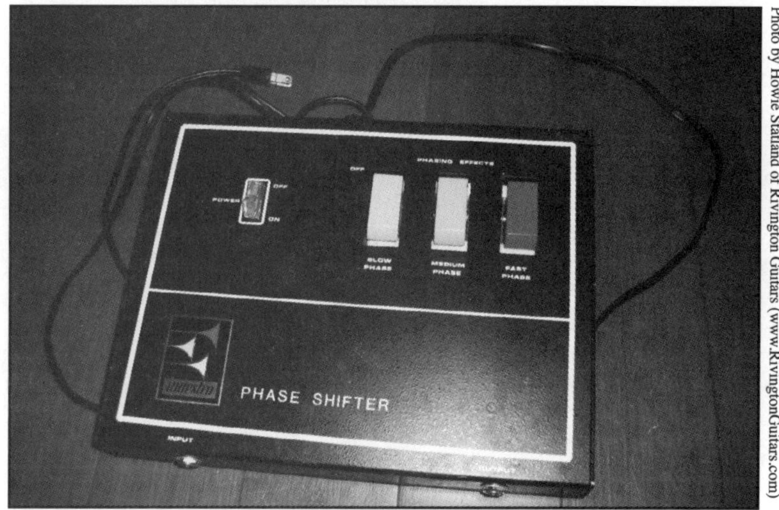

1971 Maestro PS-1 Phase Shifter.

MXR Phase 90

In 1972, MXR was formed in Rochester, New York and released its first product, the now-legendary Phase 90. The Phase 90 is probably the most popular phaser of all time due to its streamlined design and excellent tone. It can be heard prominently in the cleanly picked guitar parts on Nazareth's 1976 hit, "Love Hurts." The Phase 90 featured a single knob that controlled the rate of the sweep (the depth and resonance were internally preset to perfection). The device added a hint of grit when kicked in and came in a small, nearly indestructible die-cast housing. MXR did very well, indeed, quickly swelling to become a multi-million dollar company and releasing many additional classics like the Distortion Plus, which was favored by Randy Rhoads, and the Phase 100, which Keith Richards used on "Beast of Burden" and "Shattered" in 1978.

Other Phasers

Mutron (Musitronics) formed in Rosemont, New Jersey in 1972 and released several legendary phaser pedals such as the Mutron II and Mutron III. These indispensable funk machines added pick sensitivity to the phasing game, triggering a more vocal and wah-like effect. They could be set to sweep slowly for a typical phasing sound or function as auto-wahs.

Electro-Harmonix also entered the fray with the Small Stone, which created a crystal-clear swoosh that was much better suited for sparkling clean sounds than the gritty Phase 90. Electro-Harmonix grew quickly, offering many classics, including the Big Muff Pi fuzz and the Small Clone chorus to name a few. Their overly large, brightly painted boxes, with odd names like Soul Kiss and Screaming Tree, not only sounded great but looked wild and imparted a funky vibe.

Morley

The Morley Company, which started in the 1960s under the name of Tel-Ray Electronics, introduced a line of optically based effects that had clear advantages over their potentiometer-based counterparts in the '70s. A potentiometer, or "pot," becomes scratchy-sounding with use and eventually needs to be replaced. The tiny, inexpensive light bulb in Morley pedals was much easier to deal with, and the pedals had an appealing look, with their large steel boxes, so '70s guitarists could stand on them with their platform shoes! The 1970s Morley product line grew to include tons of cool multi-function wah-style pedals, such as the Power Wah Fuzz.

Track 12   1974 Strat, a '70s Mutron III, and a 1973 Fender Twin Reverb

1970s Morley Man logo.

Replacement Guitar Pickups: DiMarzio

DiMarzio was founded in the United States in 1972, kick-starting the replacement guitar pickup market. DiMarzio's first product was the Super Distortion pickup, which was a humbucker with a stronger magnet leading to much greater output than stock pickups of the era. True to its name, the Super Distortion could kick almost any amp into overdrive quite easily. It was a popular item and helped the company thrive.

Roland

The Roland company was formed in Japan in 1972, and its Boss division followed in 1975. The Roland Jazz Chorus amp (JC-120), released in 1975, is one of the only solid-state amps with such a unique and good sound that its tone is commonly emulated on modeling amps and software today. The rugged, powerful, and affordable JC-120 competed with Fender and Marshall by offering built-in state of the art chorusing and crystal-clear tone.

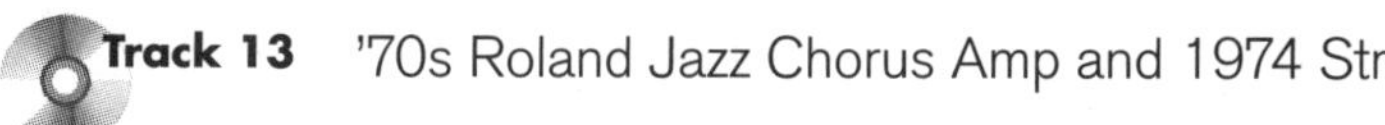 **Track 13** '70s Roland Jazz Chorus Amp and 1974 Strat

Soon, Boss pedals were flooding the market as well. Boss's intention was to make tough, durable pedals; they succeeded magnificently, and by 1976 the company offered many of the core products it still sells today, including the DS-1 Distortion, CS-1 Compressor, CE-1 Chorus Ensemble, BF-1 Flanger, PH-1 Phaser, OD-1 Overdrive, NF-1 Noise Gate, GE-6 Graphic EQ, DM-1 Delay Machine, and many more. Like MXR pedals, they were nearly indestructible and although the slightly larger footprint was a drawback, the easier battery changing was a plus.

Compressors and Limiters

Compressors and *limiters* are gain-regulating devices, which means they reduce dynamic range. A limiter prevents the signal's level from exceeding a given point or threshold. This reduction of hot levels smooths the overall response. Compressors are much more popular as guitar pedals than limiters. In addition to the limiting function, they boost low-level signals. So when a note would normally be fading away, a compressor will make it swell in volume instead. This creates highly prized sustain without distortion. The limiting function also results in a popping, percussive attack that works great for funky, clean lead guitar tones or an explosive slap bass sound.

Threshold sets the volume level above which the compressor kicks in.

Ratio determines how much the compressor turns the volume down after the input signal surpasses the threshold.

Output controls the volume coming out of the compressor. After the compressor squashes the dynamic range, use this to boost your overall level.

Ibanez

The Japanese company Ibanez has been making guitars for a very long time, but in the old days their instruments were mostly copies of other designs. Ibanez "knockoffs" of Fenders, Gibsons, and Rickenbackers hit the American market in the early '70s. This prompted a period of lawsuits that eventually resulted in Ibanez developing their own line of respectable guitar designs, such as the Iceman and the Roadstar.

Ibanez also offered a complete line of guitar effects pedals that were basically copies of MXR circuits housed in Boss-like boxes. These were high-quality units and competed well with other companies. The Ibanez story is ongoing and has resulted in several major advances, which will be covered in the next chapter. Of note, in 1979, the company scored one of its biggest hits with the introduction of a small green distortion pedal called the Tube Screamer. The pedal offered medium-gain distortion that, when combined with natural amp overdrive, really rocked!

Innovations in the Late 1970s

Almost everything was finally available to the average Joe in the 1970s. Instead of having to go to a fancy studio like Abbey Road to get your hands on a custom-built compressor unit, you could affordably purchase a stomp-box version at the local music shop. These small wonders included the MXR Dyna Comp, Electro-Harmonix Soul Preacher, Dan Armstrong Orange Squeezer, and Boss CS-1, to name a few. It would be nearly impossible to name every company that formed in the decade and all of the effects they offered.

As in the '60s, many innovations occurred in the '70s, and here are a few more highlights. The DOD Company, founded in Salt Lake City in 1974, released a full line of stomp boxes. Analog Digital Associates (ADA) was founded in 1975 by David Tarnowsky, releasing the very popular ADA Flanger in 1977.

In 1976, Peavey introduced the concepts of CNC routing and copy lathe to guitar making, methods previously only used in furniture and gun making, to produce the first truly computer-machined, precision-made musical instruments, including their T-60 model guitar. This helped evolve and streamline the manufacturing process and the same techniques were soon adopted by other companies.

Also in 1976, John Nady debuted his wireless guitar system, which started a whole industry in itself, becoming indispensable in the next decade. In 1979, Tube Works invented the first tube-driven distortion pedal, the Tube Driver. It contained a real 6AV6 tube and was an instant success, as was the Pro Co Rat distortion pedal that was released in the same year. The Rat offered everything from subtle distortion clipping to raging full-on hard rock mayhem and remains an important tone machine to this day. 1979 also marked the birth of the Tascam Portastudio. The Portastudio was a 4-track recorder that used regular cassette tapes, starting the home recording revolution that has empowered musicians ever since.

THE 1980s

The Cold War plodded on, the underpinnings of the Internet were being hashed out by the U.S. government, and global warming became known to the general public in the 1980s. Ronald Reagan was elected United States president in 1980, the same year John Lennon was killed in New York City, and the music scene was changing in reaction to unstoppable technological and cultural forces. Electro-Harmonix folded, DOD launched Digitech, and the rise of the microchip brought on MIDI-controlled rack-mounted systems instead of old-school floor pedals. As the racks grew taller, so did the hair of the artists that used them. Mullets grew like stubborn weeds as the chilling shadow of AIDS crept slowly across the land. MTV exploded in 1981 and, suddenly, everyone was sounding and looking larger-than-life right in your own living room. It wasn't necessary to fight through a stadium crowd to see artists up close anymore. The climate changed to embrace new musical genres like new wave, rap, hip-hop, and hair metal.

To make matters even more futuristic, the compact disc (CD) was made commercially available in 1982. By 1989, it was the norm and Yamaha had released the first consumer CD recorder. Orwell's *1984* date had passed without incident, but the 1980s had done its work; the digital age was here to stay and there was no turning back.

Paul Reed Smith

In 1980, as a special order for Heart guitarist Howard Leese, an Annapolis, Maryland luthier named Paul Reed Smith built a guitar he called the Golden Eagle. The instrument featured a curly maple top, which Smith had pilfered from a desk, and it signaled the start of a new direction in guitar design by combining elements of Gibsons and Fenders with ultra high-quality materials and craftsmanship (not to mention Smith's own innovative twists). By 1985, Smith had displayed his products at the NAMM show in California, helping the company become nationally known. The scale length of the Paul Reed Smith (or PRS) Custom 24 guitar, the company's early flagship, fell mid-way between that of a Gibson and a Fender at 25". The Custom 24 combined the carved top and humbuckers of a Gibson with the straight headstock pull and whammy bar of a Fender. Additional advancements included a whammy bar that stayed in tune, locking tuning pegs, and a five-position rotary switch for different pickup configurations. PRS guitars, with their translucent finishes, stunning bird-shaped inlays, and exotic woods soon landed the company the spot as America's number three guitar manufacturer, right after Gibson and Fender.

Paul Reed Smith.

Bradshaw Switching System

Bob Bradshaw formed CAE (Custom Audio Electronics) in 1980. His mission was to streamline multi-component audio systems, like pedalboards, by making switching easier and improving the sound quality. He achieved this by creating a remote switching system that activated discreet loops that contained various combinations of devices, like pedals or rack units, that were not floor-based. True bypassing of unused effects made for a better signal-to-noise ratio and housing the units in a rack made for a cleaner look on stage—as only the switcher was on the floor. Bradshaw worked for high-profile clients, creating custom Bradshaw switching systems for their rigs. He later joined forces with Rocktron to create commercially available systems. Bradshaw's ideas continue to evolve and are widely copied to this day.

Rockman X-100

Tom Scholz of the band Boston had done some pioneering work in the '70s as the producer for his own recordings. Everything about the first Boston album sounded light years ahead of its time, and when it was released in 1976 it quickly soared to the top of the charts to become the biggest-selling debut to date. The Scholz guitar sound combined distortion, compression, chorusing, and delay in just the right doses to create an awesome multi-processed sound. Scholz received a master's degree in mechanical engineering from MIT and, in 1982, bottled and corked his signature guitar tone to make it available to the public in the form of a small multiprocessor called the Rockman X-100. You could clip the unit to your belt, select from a few presets, and sound like you were in a million-dollar recording studio. Soon, the Rockman line added modular half rack units, amps, and more.

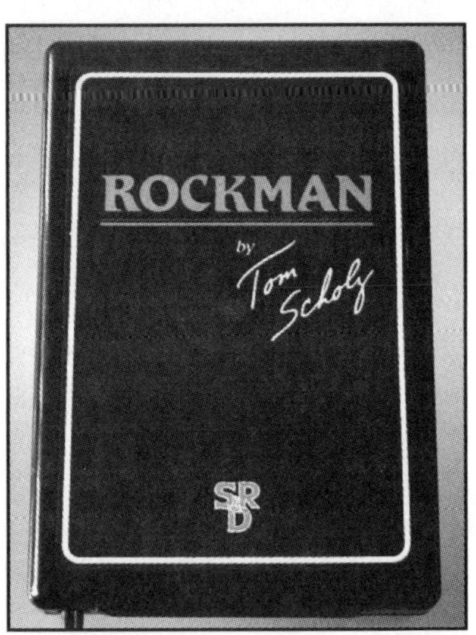

Rockman X-100.

Floyd Rose Tremolo System

The Floyd Rose double-locking tremolo system was introduced in 1982. This whammy bar system, which actually stayed in tune, pre-dated the PRS system and was a perfect tool for the army of shred-metal whammy-divers who sought to jump on the Van Halen bandwagon. (See page 79 for more on the Floyd Rose.)

Soon, new breeds of "Super Strat" guitars were being equipped with authentic Floyd Rose trems or licensed versions that worked similarly. These new axes were made by companies like Jackson, Ibanez, Kramer, and B.C. Rich, and featured high-output humbuckers with simple electronics. They met the needs of players who wanted to play loud, fast, and distorted guitar without slowing down to re-tune. Kahler released another viable take on the locking trem a year or two later, and the companies fought for market share until Floyd Rose emerged victorious in the early '90s.

Photo by Timothy Phelps

"Super Strat" with simple electronics and Floyd Rose tremolo.

MIDI

MIDI (Musical Instrument Digital Interface) was introduced in 1983. The multi-pin MIDI cable carried as many as 16 different commands from one piece of gear to another. It revolutionized the industry and coordinated sequencers, sound modules, drum machines, and recording gear for musicians and producers everywhere. For guitarists, it mostly meant that one tap of a foot switch could instantly change the settings of any number of MIDI-compatible devices that were chained together. MIDI is the reason why equipment racks grew out of control and how the "over processing" of '80s guitar tones got started. Just listen to the clean guitar part on Def Leppard's "Love Bites" for an example of over-processed guitar. MIDI technology also enabled guitar synth users to control sound modules as if their guitars were keyboards.

As soon as MIDI hit the scene, a host of companies began making MIDI-compatible rack-mounted processors of one kind or another. By the end of the 1980s, almost everyone, including ADA, Mesa/Boogie, Marshall, Digitech, Alesis, Furman, Rockman, Rocktron, Ibanez, DBX, MXR, Boss, Dunlop, Aphex, Yamaha, Eventide, Korg, and many others, offered rack-mounted gear.

Tube Preamp

Programmable tube preamps such as the ADA MP-1 were usually at the heart of any '80s guitar rack system. The MP-1 controlled the EQ, distortion, and relative volume levels with hundreds of presets that a user could save and recall. Devices like the Alesis Quadroverb and Digitech DSP 121+ were able to do four "wet" effects at once, such as combining delay, reverb, chorusing, and doubling, and this was necessary to achieve the popular sounds of the era.

Tube Power Amp

Of course, something was needed to amplify the overall sound, so a rack-mounted tube power amp was usually used with speakers of choice, usually Marshall 4x12's. The system couldn't be complete without a MIDI foot controller and a bunch of short MIDI cables and regular instrument cables to connect the units together. The controller would be connected to the MIDI input jack of the first unit and its MIDI output, or through, jack would be fed down the line to each unit until the chain was complete. All units would respond instantly to the touch of a single foot switch.

And then there were the effects with frills: the Furman Power Conditioner with little retractable lights, Nady wireless units, Hush II Noise Reduction, Dunlop remote wahs, Eventide Smart Harmonizers, and the list goes on and on. These systems either sounded great or were downright bad, depending on the acumen of the user. The programming of digital patches is still the way things are done today, except all the user needs today is a single unit, or a computer, instead of a whole rack of gear.

Overblown 1980s guitar rig.

Eventide H3000

In 1986, Eventide released the first intelligent pitch shifter, the H3000. Up until then, effects that created harmony were only able to produce parallel intervals. Intelligent harmony allowed diatonic intervals to be generated and stay in the same key signature. They could be 3rds, 6ths, or anything the user programmed. It was a major breakthrough, and suddenly single-guitar bands could play double and triple leads easily.

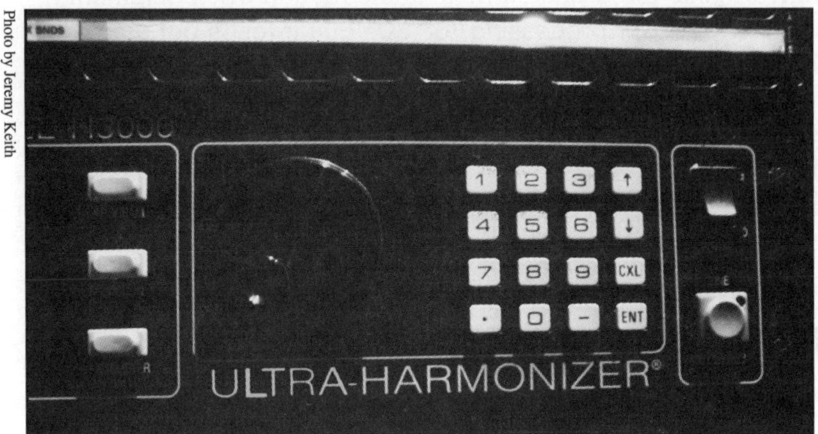

Eventide H3000 Ultra-Harmonizer.

Customizing Marshalls

The look of Marshall amps has always been important to guitar players, but the tone of the amps was a little behind the times in the '80s. The Marshall JCM-800 was an awesome and popular amp in the '80s, but it only had one channel. That's why the practice of *modding,* or customizing, Marshalls became so popular in Hollywood, California. If a player wanted the look of Marshall with the lead sound of Mesa/Boogie, he would simply have an extra preamp tube, or two, added to get that cascading high-gain tone and a foot-switch jack installed to get channel switching from a JCM-800. Even though this may seem silly now, it was the norm at the time.

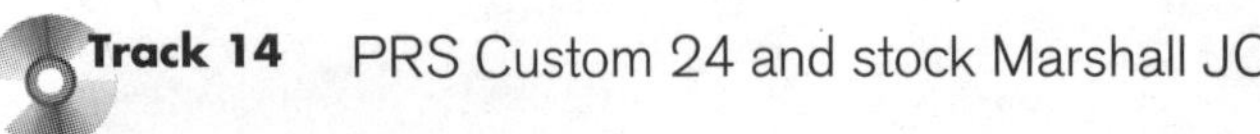

Track 14   PRS Custom 24 and stock Marshall JCM-800

7-String Note: *In previous decades, the use of 7-string guitars was largely relegated to jazz pioneers like George Van Eps, but in the early '80s Scorpions axeman Uli Jon Roth began sniffing around at the idea and devised his 7-string Sky guitar. He may have influenced Ibanez, who by the mid-1980s had all but cornered the market on shred guitars. Steve Vai, Paul Gilbert, and Joe Satriani all endorsed Ibanez, and soon Vai would be playing the Ibanez 7-string Universe guitar. Vai played the prototypes in 1989 and used the Universe on his 1990 album* Passion and Warfare *and on his tour with Whitesnake.*

Double and Quad Guitars

In 1989, shred-metal guitarist Michael Angelo Batio was seen on MTV with the band Nitro playing his self-invented, custom-made Quad guitar, which included four necks. The two top necks had seven strings, and the bottom two had six strings. Batio patented the special string dampers that were fitted to this instrument as well as to his self-invented Double guitar. At around the same time, guitarists Jennifer Batten and Stanley Jordan also experimented with string dampers to facilitate their two-handed tapping techniques.

Photo courtesy of Michael Angelo Batio

Michael Angelo Batio with two Dean Double guitars.

SansAmp

In 1989, the New York company Tech 21 created a product called the SansAmp. It was the first direct recording device that simulated different amps and went on to usher in the new age of amp modeling. Future companies, like Line 6, would owe their business model to this major innovation that SansAmp had developed. Meanwhile, a Seattle, Washington band called Nirvana released their first album in 1989. It was called *Bleach*.

THE 1990s

The 1990s were a time of relative peace and prosperity for the United States. When the Soviet Union fell in 1991, the Cold War was officially over, leaving the United States as the last one standing, clearly the world's leading superpower. Bill Clinton was elected U.S. president in 1992, and though his presidency was tainted by the Monica Lewinsky scandal, he balanced the budget and helped the economy thrive.

Internet sites began popping up in the early '90s and multiplied steadily until 1995 when the restrictions on commercial traffic were lifted, allowing major, unprecedented expansion of the Internet. No one could have predicted its endless variety and vast sociopolitical impact. Among the earliest music sites were, of course, MTV, but there was also something that MTV probably didn't like very much: IUMA, or Internet Underground Music Archive. There were no program directors at IUMA and no A&R men. Anyone could get international exposure as a musician, and the Website paid mechanical royalties. Players didn't necessarily get rich from IUMA, as some only received checks for around 12 cents, but a new distribution model, that would eventually kill the audio CD, was in place. When the MP3 format was standardized in 1994, it became inevitable.

The tides of the music industry turned again in the '90s, with the grunge movement sparking a return to basic songwriting and straightforward equipment. Hair metal and all its excess withered, as a burgeoning "retro-trend" reignited interest in simple stomp boxes and combo amps.

A new industry was forming, led by the development of boutique amps and pedals, which featured small batches of handcrafted units with an old-school vibe and funky new features. As amp modeling squared off against tubes, the decade showed its split personality—with one side going technical and the other retro.

Pro Tools

The first version of the Pro Tools recording software was released in 1991. It offered only four tracks and was extremely expensive, but soon the features began to multiply and the price dropped. This helped lead to the advent of *plug-ins,* which are aftermarket software programs that can be combined with recording software, such as Pro Tools, to act like effects pedals or processors. They can be chained together to achieve various combinations of sounds just like pedals. The use of plug-ins allowed guitar tones to be changed in the mixdown, instead of being printed permanently to tape. The first widely popular guitar amp simulation plug-in was Line 6's Amp Farm, released in 1998.

Matchless

In 1991, the Matchless boutique amp company started in Hollywood, California, and by 1992 their acclaimed DC-30 2x12" combo was featured alongside mainstream combo amps from Fender, Crate, Yamaha, Peavey, Carvin, Marshall, and Vox in a *Guitar Player* magazine article. The major manufacturers felt the heat, eventually responding with "faithful" reissues of their own vintage amps.

Track 15   1992 Fender Stratocaster into Budda Superdrive Half Stack

Digitech Whammy Pedal

Digitech scored a major hit in around 1991 with the release of the Whammy pedal. Just when it seemed like all the good ideas had already been taken, the Whammy came along and created sounds never heard before. Guitarists like Joe Satriani and Tom Morello had fun rocking the pedal to the toe position which blasted their riffs an octave higher. It's an awesome sound and the Whammy has become a mainstay on many a pedalboard ever since.

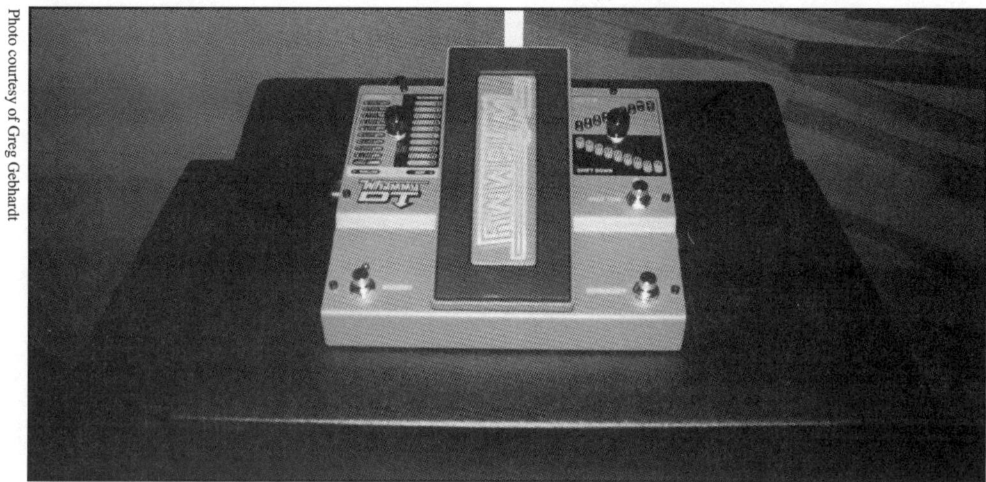

Digitech Whammy pedal.

Parker Fly

In 1992, Ken Parker started Parker Guitars, and by 1993, he and Ken Fishman had developed the company's flagship guitar, the Parker Fly. The sleek and modern Fly weighed in at only 4.5 pounds and featured traditional magnetic as well as piezoelectric pickups, allowing access to both acoustic and electric tones, or the combination of both at once. The Fly featured a body composed of a carbon fiber/glass/epoxy material. The unique design and materials made the lightweight body rigid and helped the guitar sustain longer. The clean sound and playability of the Parker Fly remain extraordinary to this day, though its distorted tones may lack the warmth and complexity of traditional guitars.

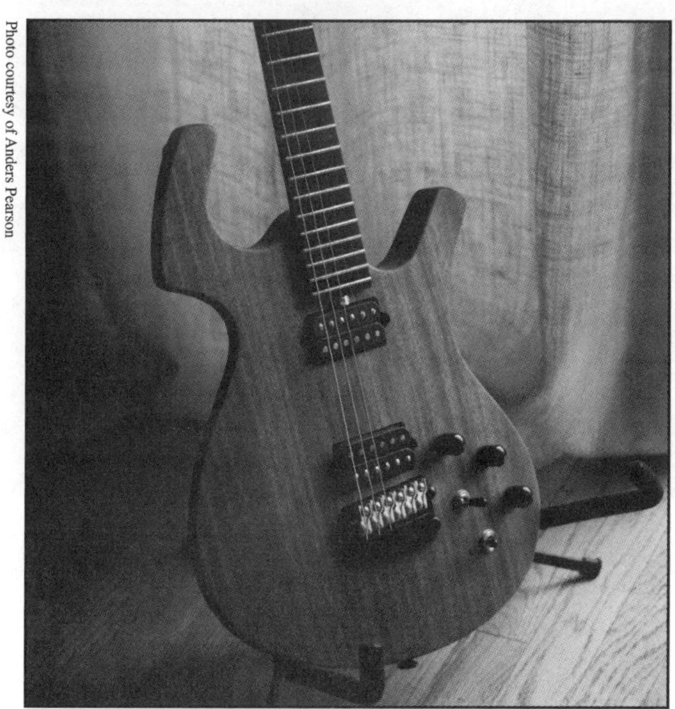

Parker Fly guitar.

Grunge Pedal

The repackaging and renaming of old technology became commonplace in the '90s. In 1993, DOD released the extremely popular Grunge pedal. It was simply a fuzz box that said "grunge" on it, and Kurt Cobain's only use of it was to throw it into the crowd at a live show. The device was discontinued, later re-issued, and has now even been modeled.

7-String Note: When Korn used 7-string Ibanez Universe guitars on their 1994 debut, the 7-string craze was officially on. It was not only Korn and Steve Vai, though, since Limp Bizkit, Dream Theater, Joey Tafolla, Fear Factory, Lacuna Coil, Meshuggah, and many other '90s players made music on seven strings. Soon, artists of this ilk began playing signature models with special features like a longer scale length, active pickups, and heavy strings. These adjustments helped the 7th string produce a more stable pitch. The idea was to get massive low-end rumble out of the guitar, so everyone tuned down way below normal and it became necessary to take great pains to stop the 7th string from fretting out and loosely flopping around like a rubber band. It didn't always work, but those who took the time and effort achieved the goal.

Ibanez K7 Korn Model signature guitar.

Sovtek

Mike Matthews, perhaps spurred on by the re-awakened interest in stomp boxes, started New Sensor Corporation in 1996. They sold Russian-made reissues of classic Electro-Harmonix pedals like the Big Muff. New Sensor also owned Sovtek, which had a line of amps fitted with Matthew's Russian-made tubes. The tubes were equivalent to 12AX7, EL34, 6L6, and EL84 tubes. Since tube manufacturing had died out in the United States due to dwindling demand, high costs, and environmental impact, it was a no-brainer for Matthews to oversee his factory at a time when tubes were only being made in Russia, China, and Japan. He imported them back to the U.S. where they found homes in a huge variety of audio equipment. Eventually, the Electro-Harmonix brand started releasing new products and returned to its former brightly painted glory.

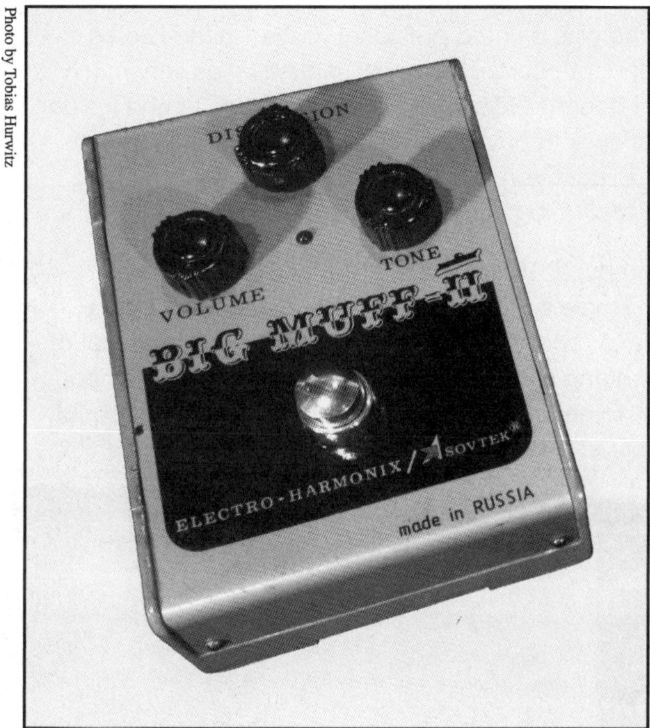

Photo by Tobias Hurwitz

Russian made Big Muff.

Innovations in the Late 1990s

Despite all the retro-trending, MIDI programmable units continued to march forward in the 1990s. Marshall offered the JMP-1 tube preamp and Mesa had the Triaxis. Both were amazingly versatile tone machines, and when paired with outboard gear, like Eventide's new Ultra-Harmonizer, the package was complete. Diehard metal heads who had stayed true to the previous decade's tonal aesthetics were in tone heaven!

By 1999, computers and the Internet had become so prevalent that the thought of a major glitch prompted by the Y2K scare made New Year's Eve seem even more apocalyptic than Prince had painted it. In the new millennium, the battle between tubes and digital modeling would continue to rage.

2000 AND BEYOND

The 21st century began with a collective sigh of relief as the Y2K scare amounted to nothing. But, right after George W. Bush was elected U.S. president in 2000, the September 11th attacks in 2001 threw the world into a state of chaos. The War on Terror was declared, and it seemed things would never be the same. The Internet had completely taken over the world, along with cell phones and social media. Everyone was recording on computer-based systems and digital distribution was king. Very few people seemed to buy music or movies. Of course, there were the exceptions of seeing a movie on the big screen or attending a live concert, but this shift drove up ticket and merchandise prices. Meanwhile, the guitar overtook the piano as the most popular instrument in the U.S. and remains so to date.

A period of global economic recession began in 2007 and took a particularly sharp downward turn in September 2008. When Barack Obama was elected president of the United States in 2009, the world economy was in shambles and, of course, the music industry was very much affected. When the financial firm Bain Capital bought Guitar Center, the fat was cut and insider discounts stopped. Older companies like Morley sold off assets, such as Accutronics Reverb, and it seemed like no one would invest in anything. Even huge chains like Borders bookstores disappeared. Though times got tough, music technology and innovation marched on.

In 2003, the iTunes music store was born, and by 2009 it had emerged triumphantly, commanding 70% of music sales worldwide. Apple's iPod music player was just as popular, and the new trend among pop musicians was to record either a click track or their entire set of music on an iPod and have the drummer play along with it to keep the band in perfect tempo. Car and home stereos became iPod-enabled. Even the cartoonish guitarist Buckethead could be seen on stage using an iPod to control his backing tracks.

Buckethead plays to an iPod backing track without a band.

Amp Modeling

Amp-modeling technology was moving fast, with Line 6 in the lead. In 2006, Boss introduced COSM (Composite Object Sound Modeling), Roland's proprietary version of digital modeling technology. This was built into the Boss's GT floor-based pedal line and also Roland's excellent Cube amps. Vox introduced Valvetronix, which combined a real 12AX7 tube with digital modeling technology. Marshall released the JDM-100, a fully programmable amp-modeling head in 2010.

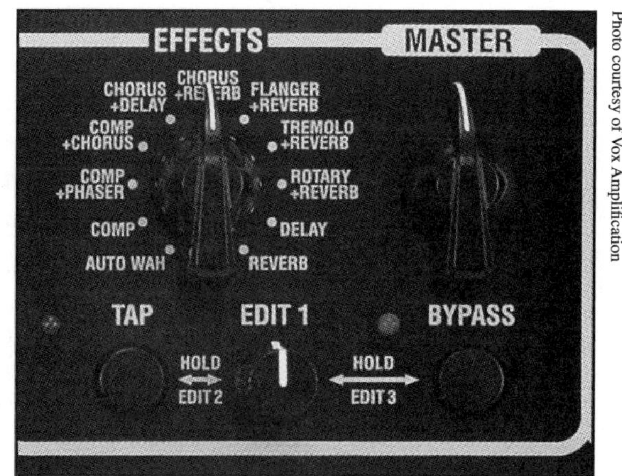

FX selector on Vox DA15 modeling amp.

Photo courtesy of Vox Amplification

Guitar Apps

Apps have helped smart phones and other mobile devices dominate the modern era. With an electric guitar plugged in via an adapter, like the iRig from IK Multimedia, an iPhone or Android phone (or iPad or Android tablet) could function as a little recording studio, amp modeler, stomp box, phrase trainer, ear-training quizzer, metronome, and tuner—almost anything a guitarist could ask for. Even though things have come this far, many players still don't want to spend their time programming. Let's face it, for many of us, it's still easier to just plug into a combo amp and play!

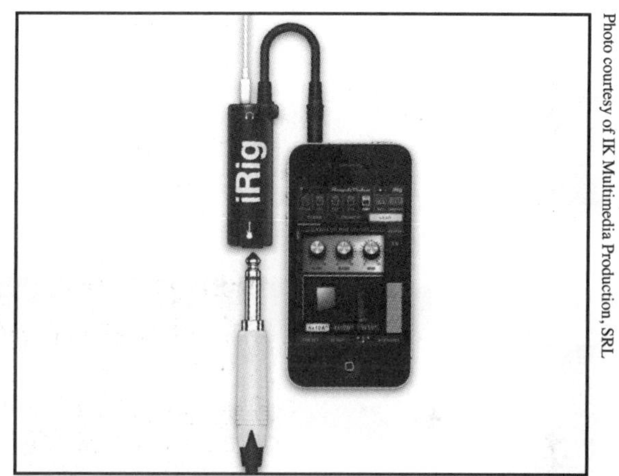

iRig adapter and iPhone.

Photo courtesy of IK Multimedia Production, SRL

8- and 9-String Guitars

Though the awesome Morpheus Drop Tune pedal allows players to get the lowest sounds possible from a regular six-string guitar, without any off-color tones or the usual problems inherent with 7-string guitars, now we have 8- and 9-string guitars. Why? These "extended-range" instruments could go even lower.

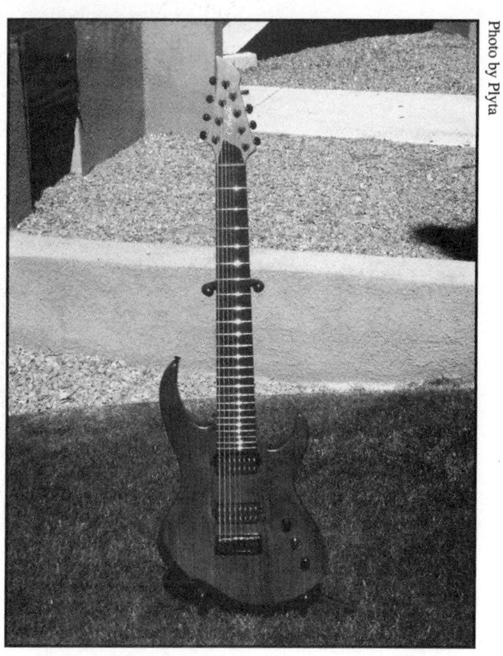

Agile Intrepid 8-string guitar.

Photo by Plyta

Guitar-Based Video Games

In 2005, electronic entertainment company RedOctane released the *Guitar Hero* video game, and suddenly there was vast renewed interest in guitars and guitar-driven music. *Guitar Hero* was followed by the *Rock Band* video game by Harmonix, and perhaps even inspired Ubisoft's 2012 game *Guitarsmith*, which allowed the user to plug in a real electric guitar and play! These fun inventions provided a much needed shot in the arm for recession-weary music merchandisers everywhere!

Look, Ma, No Amp!

In the post-2000 era, there was a growing movement away from amp dependence. Many players, such as Misha Mansoor of Periphery, didn't use amps at all any more and simply plugged a studio-grade modeling processor straight into the P.A. system or the monitors of a home recording studio. This eliminated the need for amps, pedals, speakers, and microphones.

The device of choice of tech-savvy tone geeks appeared to be all-in-one units that could serve as a live direct box, an interface to a computer environment, a multi-effects processor, and an amp modeler. Many such devices exist, including the Fractal Audio Systems Axe-FX released in 2006, Digidesign 11 Rack in 2009, and Digitech iPB-10 released in 2010. The iPB-10 acts as a docking and control station for the Apple iPad. All of these units are powerful tools for the modern guitarist and provide a vast array of features and capabilities, which may sometimes not be easily accessible without considerable effort on the part of the user. That said, the younger the user, the easier the job, usually—due to the increasing familiarity with computer-based technologies by younger users.

Fractal Audio Systems Axe-FX II

So where has nearly 100 years of electric guitar tone evolution finally led us to in the 2010s? The Fractal Audio Systems Axe-FX II, now in its 3rd generation, has risen to the top as, arguably, the best all-in-one guitar rig available. It's a two-space rack unit that can be connected to any computer via a USB cable, so editing can be done on a full-sized screen or on the unit's front panel LED display. Two kinds of software are used with the Axe-FX II: Firmware, which is the software onboard the unit, and Axe Edit, which must be downloaded to a computer and is used to program the unit and organize the patches. The software evolves very quickly, and updated versions of both are released frequently. The downloading and installation of these updates adds more features and better tone quality to the unit. This is the result of a fast-moving R&D (research and development) team and constant feedback from active online user forums, where players swap patches, ask each other questions, report bugs, and request new features from Fractal. Historically, a new physical unit was released when the CPU power of the old version could no longer handle the demands of the new software.

Photo courtesy of Fractal Audio Systems

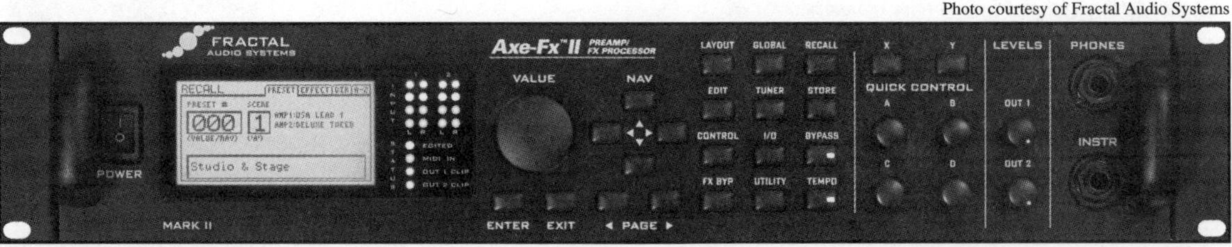

Fractal Audio Systems Axe-FX II.

Virtually any pedal, microphone, speaker cabinet, amp, or outboard unit can be modeled in breathtaking detail with the Axe-FX II. They can be put in any order and four lengthy stereo chains can be combined and mixed to perfection for multi-amp scenarios and tone blending. The Axe-FX II also contains a looper, a tuner, and a full complement of programmable inputs and outputs for versatile digital and analog connectivity.

Fractal Audio's MFC-101 foot controller is a major innovation in its own right. As the companion to the Axe-FX II, the MFC-101 features a clear, bright LCD display that is plainly visible even in full sunlight. The display adjusts automatically to the amount of ambient or direct light and always looks the same. The MFC-101 is connected via an Ethernet cable, which carries power to the unit as well as all of the data. This easy hook-up makes for a clean look onstage, with no wall wart. The unit has 21 buttons with bright dual-function LEDs, jacks for four additional expression pedals, and two additional two-button foot switches. Of course, users must learn to program the MFC-101 if they wish to take advantage of all of this.

Fractal Audio Systems MFC-101 foot controller.

Looking Ahead

So where does it go from here? Only time will tell. The great ideas may seem fewer and farther in between than they were in previous decades, but innovations still keep coming no matter what. In 2013, Boss released an "adaptive" distortion pedal that reacts to the range of the notes being played and maintains clarity throughout the entire fretboard. Also in 2013, D'Addario introduced balanced-tension strings which allowed players to apply the same amount of pressure to each string, making playing, and bending in particular, feel the same on every string. And there are those new rechargeable, small-footprint pedals made by Red Witch... It goes on and on.

PART 2: A CLOSE LOOK AT THE ELECTRIC GUITAR

UNDERSTANDING THE ELECTRIC GUITAR

It's amazing how much there is to know about an electric guitar. Even experienced players sometimes get hazy when it comes to finer points like scale length, fretboard radius, and fret shape. Below, you'll find two diagrams of electric guitars with their basic parts labeled. Studying these illustrations will help familiarize you with the parts that will be discussed in upcoming sections.

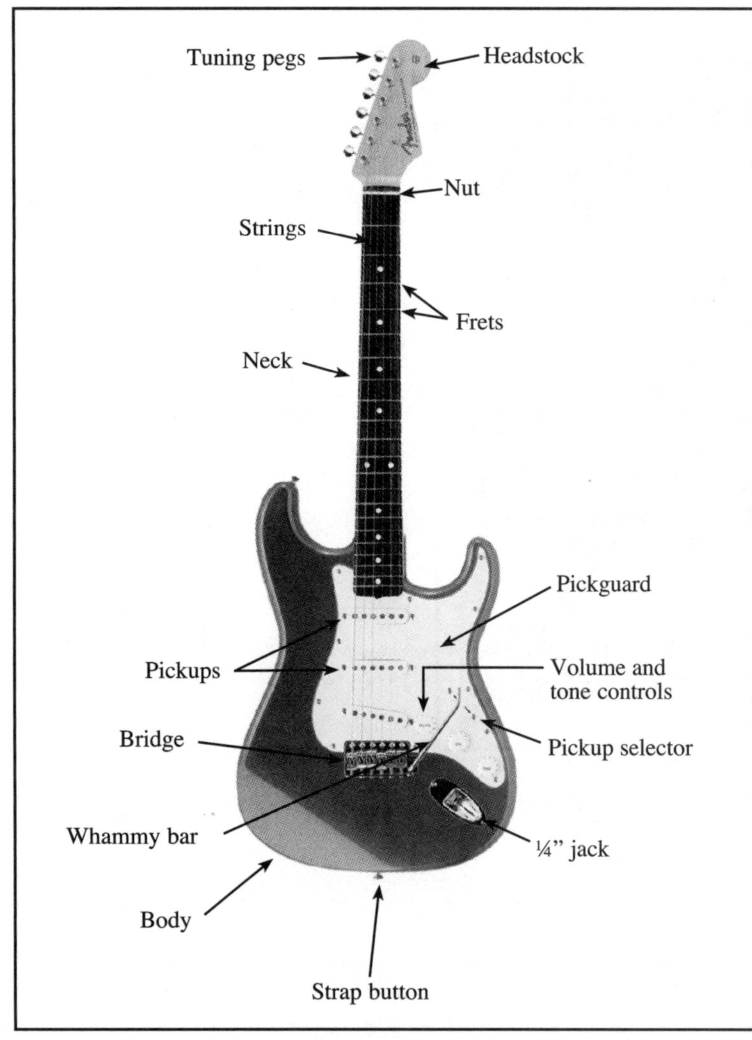

Fender Stratocaster with parts labeled.

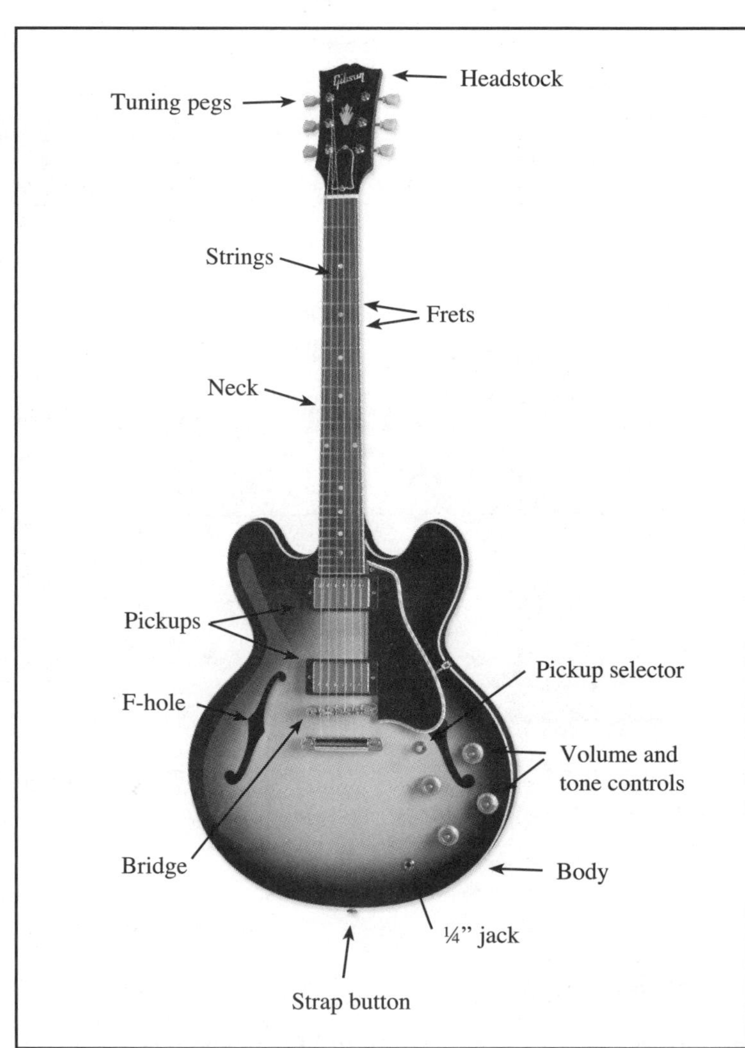

Gibson ES-335 with parts labeled.

STRINGS

Strings can make or break any guitar. If you let them get too old, fretted notes can end up sounding a half step, or more, flat. Buzzing and other problematic sounds can often be fixed simply by changing the strings. Assuming that you have fresh strings, it still makes a huge difference which kind you use. For instance, you'll never sound like Charlie Christian with light-gauge strings, and you'll never sound like Eddie Van Halen with heavy ones. Let's discuss several aspects of the string itself to better understand the situation.

Gauge

String *gauge* (thickness) is measured in thousandths of an inch, and sets of guitar strings are often referred to by the measurement of the high-E string. For instance, if the 1st string (high-E string) in a set of guitar strings is 0.009", then the set is referred to as a 9-gauge set or, simply, a set of 9s. Most electric guitars come from the factory strung with 9s. This generally means the six strings are the following gauges:

1st String	2nd String	3rd String	4th String	5th String	6th String
.009"	.011"	.016"	.024"	.032"	.042"

A 9-gauge set of guitar strings may be called "light" or "super slinky," depending on the manufacturer. Below is a table showing the most common electric guitar string set gauges.

1st String	2nd String	3rd String	4th String	5th String	6th String
.008"	.011"	.014"	.022"	.030"	.038"
.009"	.011"	.016"	.024"	.032"	.042"
.010"	.013"	.017"	.026"	.036"	.046"
.011"	.014"	.018"	.028"	.038"	.048"
.012"	.016"	.020"	.032"	.042"	.054"
.013"	.017"	.026"	.036"	.046"	.056"

The table above doesn't reflect every string-gauge combination. Manufacturers also offer "hybrid" sets that combine the first three strings from one set with the last three of an adjacent one, so for example the high strings of a 9-gauge set are combined with the low strings of a 10-gauge set. This creates a "light top, heavy bottom" effect. The idea is to create a string set that offers a beefy low-end sound but also facilitates easy string bending.

String gauge affects playability and tone. The lighter the string, the easier it is to press down and to bend, but the overall sound will also be thinner. It makes sense that the fatter the string, the fatter the tone; listen to Stevie Ray Vaughan, who used 13-gauge strings, for a perfect example. Eric Clapton and George Harrison used light-gauge strings as they were interested in bending more easily and didn't mind the trade-off in tone. Many players who use heavy strings opt to tune down a half step, which will decrease string tension, making it easier to bend and leading to a much fatter sound.

TYPES OF STRING WINDINGS

Roundwound

On a typical set of electric guitar strings, the 1st, 2nd, and 3rd strings are unwound, while the rest are wound. In some heavier-gauge sets, the 3rd string will also be wound. In most cases, the core wire is round with another round wire wrapped around it. This is called a *roundwound* string and is used by most rock, pop, and blues players. The exterior round wire that wraps around the core string creates a bit of texture on the surface of the string, resulting in a bright sound that produces some string rasp while sliding (of course, this works really well for pick slides).

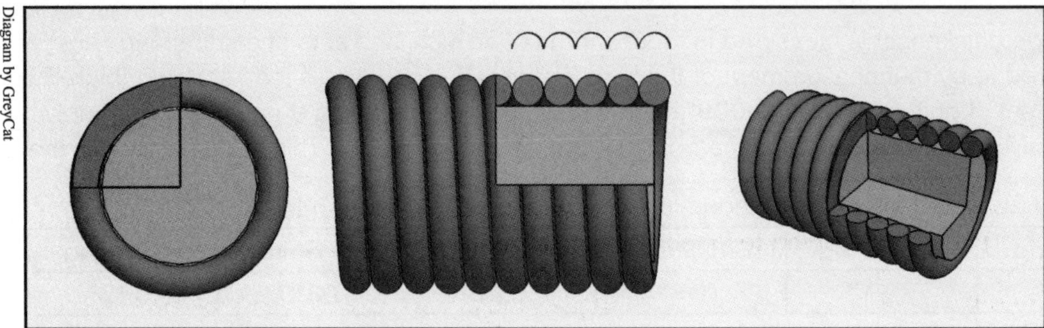

Diagram of a roundwound string.

Flatwound

Another type of winding is called *flatwound,* where the exterior winding is done with a flat wire instead of a round one. Flatwounds are preferred by jazz players because they reduce string rasp and result in a comparatively "dead" sound. The player's finger glides more easily across the string's smooth surface on flatwound strings.

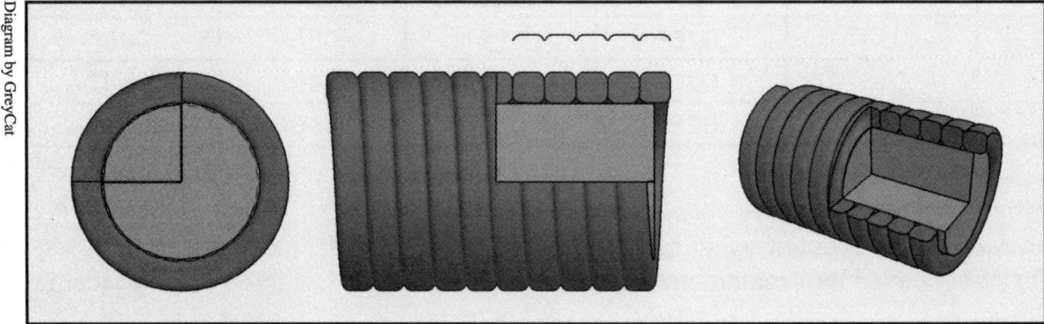

Diagram of a flatwound string.

Half Roundwound and Quarter Roundwound

There are several varieties of partially flattened wrapping wires, including *half roundwound* and *quarter roundwound* strings. These feature shallower crevices in between the wrappings, bridging the gap between round and flatwound strings to give players more options to choose from.

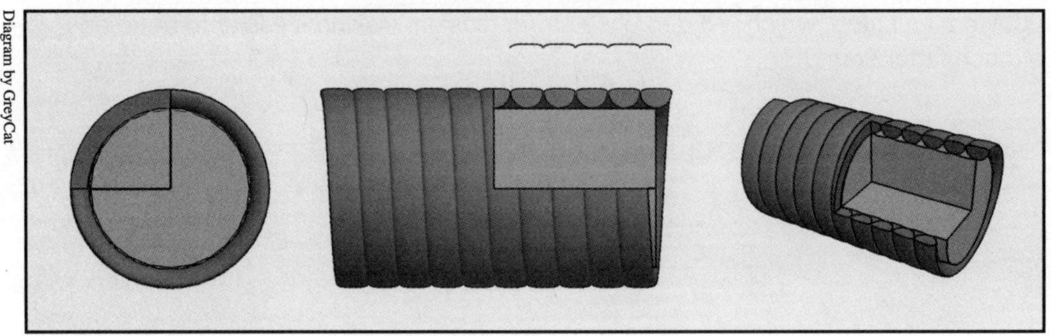

Diagram of half roundwound string.

Materials

Ernie Ball's "Regular Slinky" electric guitar strings feature a nickel-plated steel wire wrapped around a tin-plated, hex-shaped steel core wire. The tin plating helps fight corrosion, which will easily shorten the life of guitar strings. Ernie Ball's practice of using hex-shaped core wires is somewhat unusual though. The core wire most commonly used by string manufacturers, including D'Addario, Dean Markley, and DR, is a round, solid steel wire. The wrapping is most commonly nickel-plated steel, or in some cases pure nickel. Though, hexagonal core wire is also offered by D'Addario, among others, in select packs. Ernie Ball also makes strings that feature a solid steel core wrapped with a unique iron/cobalt alloy. Cobalt players claim the strings offer better sustain and punch, and last longer.

Ball End

The ball end of a string makes a huge difference in quality, mostly because that's where a string usually breaks. Therefore, the method of attachment is very important. Bargain strings tend to have poorly attached ends that break quite easily. Of course, major brands generally do a better job of attaching the ends, leading to longer-lasting strings.

In addition, the ball end may differ from one string manufacturer to another. Ernie Ball offers the option of reinforced ball ends for longer string life. D'Addario color codes the ends of their strings for easier identification since their eco-friendly packaging doesn't individually wrap each string. Fender offers a "bullet" end, which is heavier and larger, to create more sustain, Fender claims.

Coated Strings

String coating is a relatively recent development. Elixir was the first company to manufacture coated strings, and by 2000 they had swept the market. Elixir's process involves coating the string with a thin, evenly applied insulating plastic-like substance. The coating seals the string, preventing moisture, such as sweat and skin oil, to set in and corrode the string. Depending on the string manufacturer, the various materials used to coat strings include polymers and Teflon-like materials. With the extra materials involved in manufacturing, coated strings are usually priced a bit higher than conventional strings. And, bear in mind, only the wound strings are usually coated.

As we all know, the rusted string is a tone-destroying abomination that must be avoided. So, the coated string is obviously the answer, right? They certainly do last longer, which is why so many acoustic guitars come strung with them straight from the factory even though they are a little more expensive. Since the gaps on the string surface created in the wrapping process are partially filled by the coating, string rasp and fret wear are reduced. But when the string begins to wear out, little shards of the coating material will start to dangle off the string. This may not be quite as bad as rust, but it's fairly annoying.

There are other factors to consider with coated strings. The strings will feel a little slippery and impart a slightly different tone. It's hard to pin down the difference, but the resulting tone change seems to lend itself better to acoustic than to electric playing. Electric guitarists might consider just buying less expensive conventional strings and changing them more frequently.

Illustrations by Hoe Hsin Loong/City Music Co. Pte. Ltd.

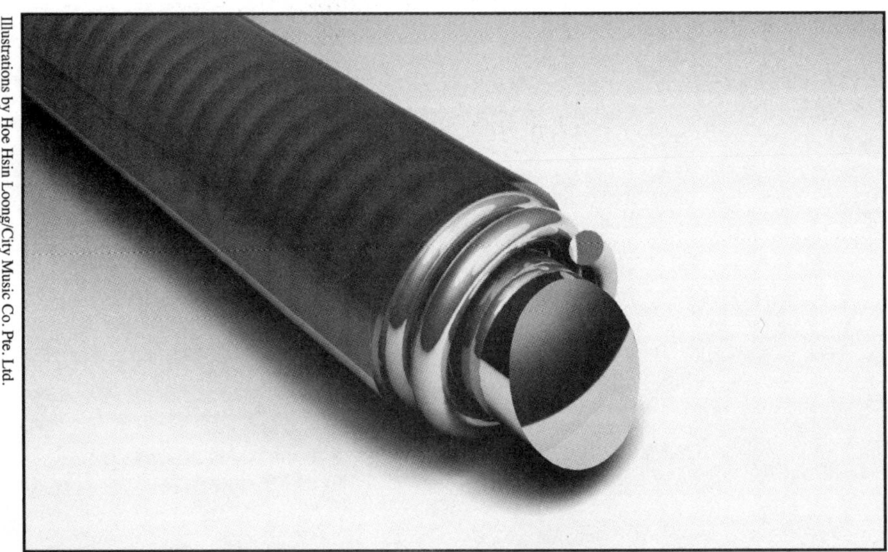

Coated wound string.

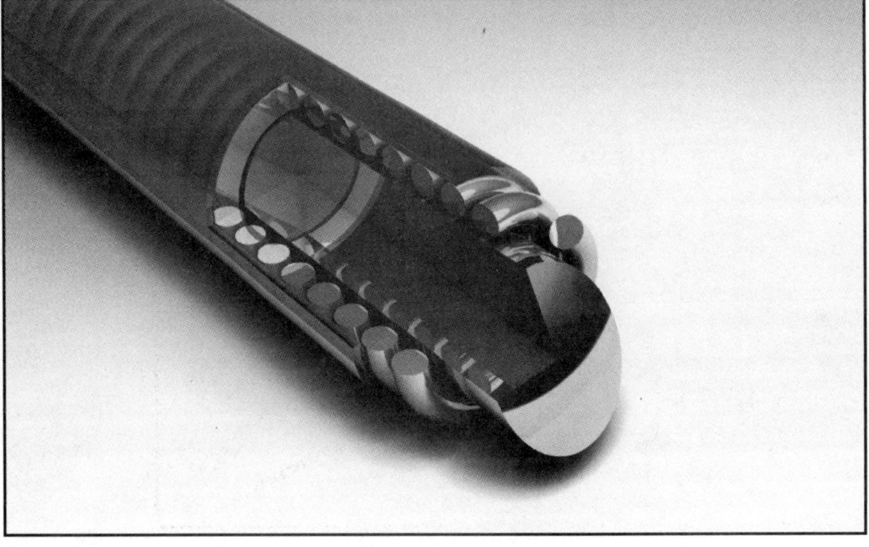

Cross-section view of coated wound string.

PICKUPS

A guitar *pickup* is essentially a magnet with six metal pole pieces wrapped in wire. There have been many design variations, such as additional pole pieces, multiple magnets, additional winding, onboard battery amplification, and more, but the basic design and concept has remained the same through the years. The vibrations of a guitar string pass through a magnetic field and are converted into electronic signals that are then sent to an amplifier through an instrument cable. Pickups come in three basic categories: single-coil, humbucking, and active.

Photo by Jan Krömer

The vibrations of a guitar string pass through a magnetic field (above) and are converted into electronic signals that are then sent to an amplifier through an instrument cable (below).

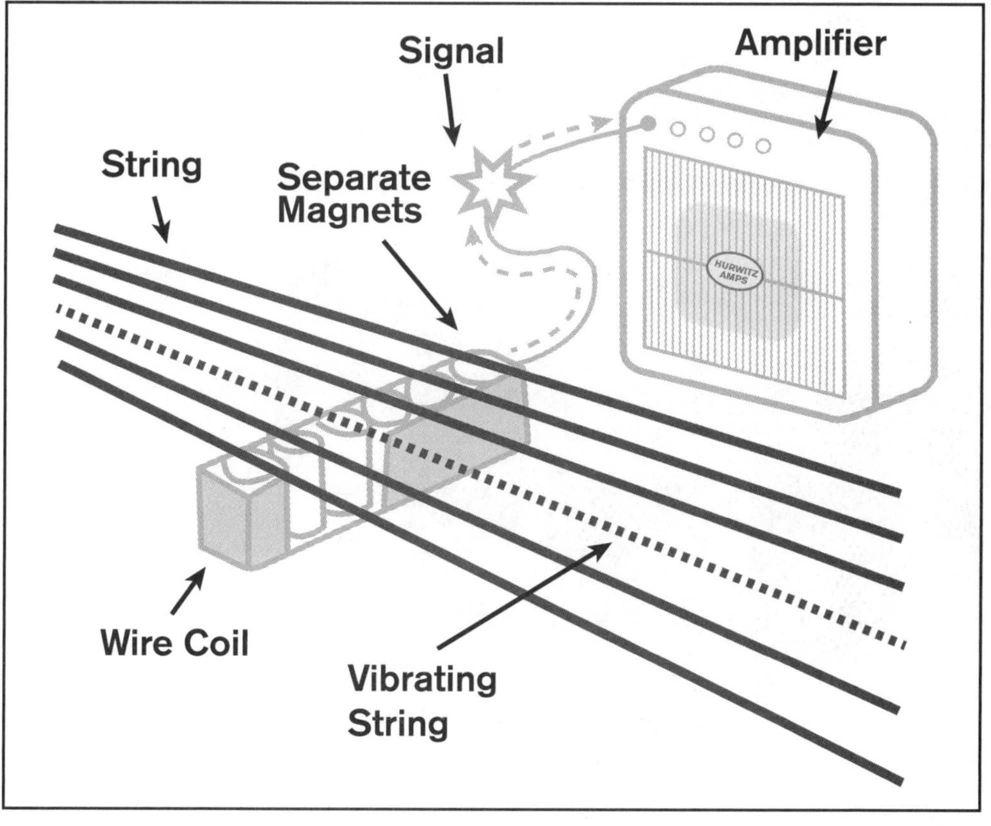

Single-Coil Pickups

The *single-coil* pickup is the original electric guitar pickup. George Beauchamp pioneered this design in the mid-1920s while moving toward creating the first solid-body electric guitar, the "Frying Pan." (See Page 5 for full details.)

The average single-coil pickup produces a relatively low volume output signal with a fair amount of hum in it. If a guitarist is using clean or low-gain tones, then this isn't a problem. Think clean funk, blues, and rock rhythm guitar tones. Listen to Jimi Hendrix's intro to "Little Wing" for an example of the sound. Additional well-known single-coil players include Charlie Christian, David Gilmour, Stevie Ray Vaughan, Eric Clapton, and Yngwie Malmsteen.

Today's single-coil pickups range from the full, warm sound of the Gibson-style P-90 to the buzzy chime of the vintage Strat-style version. The single-coil tone has a certain clarity and purity that is unmatched by any other pickup. Modern single-coils are also available in noiseless quiet models that function beautifully in high-gain situations.

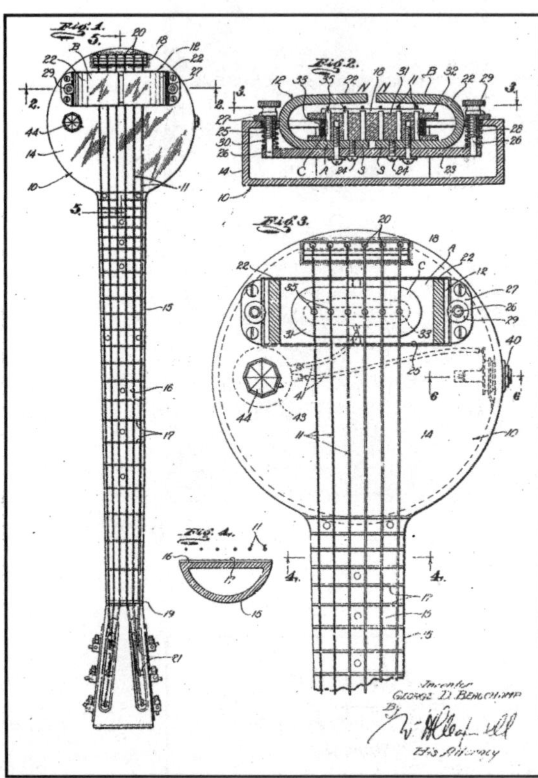

Diagram of Beauchamp's "Frying Pan" lap steel guitar from his 1934 patent application.

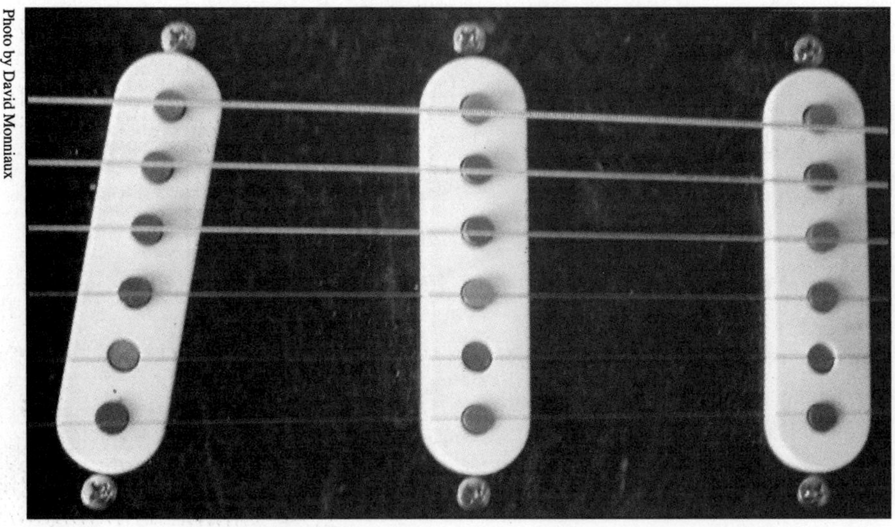

Modern single-coil pickups.

Humbucking Pickups

Humbucking pickups, also called double-coil pickups or simply humbuckers, are commonly found on Gibson-style and other electric guitars that are designed to produce louder, darker, and potentially higher-gain sounds. The humbucker uses two coils to "buck the hum" (or cancel out the interference), induced by the alternating current in single-coil pickups; the resulting humbucker is louder and considerably less noisy than single-coil pickups. The humbucking sound can be used for anything from clean, fat jazz tones to classic rock and heavy metal.

Open-coil (uncovered) humbucking pickups.

Covered humbuckers.

Humbucker devotees include Joe Pass, George Benson, Les Paul, B. B. King, Jimmy Page, Frank Zappa, Slash, Eddie Van Halen, and many others. Listen to the intro to "Sweet Child o' Mine" by Guns N' Roses for an example of the humbucker distortion sound.

Active Pickups

Active pickups are battery-powered electromagnetic pickups that amplify a guitar's signal to send out a higher gain signal to the amplifier. They come in many varieties, including some that feature active equalizers or filters for extra tone shaping. Active pickups have several advantages, compared to other pickups: they are virtually noiseless, have better sustain, and the tone doesn't change when you turn the volume down. Since they are about 95% less magnetic than regular pickups, they never generate unpleasant tones by being set too close to the strings, nor are they susceptible to noise generated by being close to light fixtures—as you would with non-active pickups, also known as *passive* pickups. EMG is the most popular brand for active pickups. The convenient thing with EMGs is once a guitar is wired for them, they can easily be switched to other EMG pickups without having to solder wires.

Most modern bass guitars have active pickups as do most acoustic-electric guitars. Heavy metal guitarists tend to prefer active pickups because they deliver more distortion, therefore 7- and 8-string guitars often come standard with active pickups.

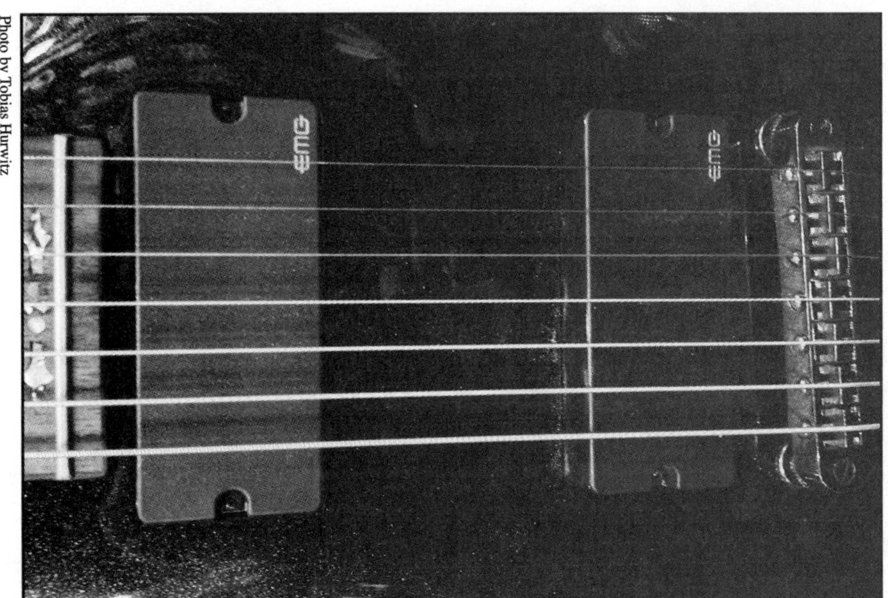

7-String Schecter Diamond Series with active EMG Pickups.

When an instrument cable is plugged into the output jack of a guitar equipped with active pickups, the 9-volt battery onboard is always running, whether or not the guitar is being played. So, it's important to remember to unplug your guitar when you're not playing. The 9-volt battery onboard should last from six months to a year, unless it is drained prematurely by keeping the cable plugged in.

It seems like active pickups have many benefits, so why doesn't everyone use them? There could be a few reasons. First, high-profile active pickup users, like David Gilmour and Metallica, attract a lot of attention and might influence many players to get into active pickups. But, players of their stature have guitar techs who handle the maintenance of constantly changing batteries. It's easy for the high-profile guitarists to enjoy the benefits without the hassles. The average kid who buys a bass with an active pickup installed is another story. He might not even know it needs batteries until his tone has gradually degenerated into an anemic, noisy, distorted mess. Then, it completely cuts out.

Then there's the higher output situation. Though a small percentage of active pickups deliver moderate output levels, these are few and far between. Guitar amps, pedals, and processors react very differently to varying amounts of input gain. Frankly, they're usually designed to function normally and correctly with the signal of a passive pickup. A passive single-coil pickup yields a crystal-clear tone and a passive bridge-position humbucker might just start to break up, but an active pickup would almost certainly overdrive an amp. It may be difficult to get a crystal-clear, undistorted tone from an active pickup without turning the volume knob down slightly on the guitar.

Handwound Pickups

Even in the old days of pickup manufacturing, circa the 1950s, pickups weren't wrapped by hand, so the term "handwound" may be a little misleading. To make a pickup, an operator would guide a wire into place as the machine wrapped it around the magnet; there are generally between 5,000 to 10,000 wraps of hair-thin copper wire. This slightly unpredictable process created pickups that were anything but consistent. Varying degrees of tightness or looseness in the coil, differing numbers of wraps per coil, crossed wires, and other anomalies were involved in the making of pickups of the same make, model, and year. The resulting pickups could sound freakishly great, though were often just average and even subpar. Consistency was not a hallmark of pickup manufacturing in the old days.

Modern manufacturing techniques allow for consistent pickup winding, which means all of the pickups for a particular make, model, and year will sound virtually identical. Improved performance can be systematically engineered instead of being happened upon by chance. Nonetheless, many players still swear by handwound pickups. They are definitely unique, and if you get a good one, no one else will have exactly the same tone as you!

Pickup-winding station.

New coil winding on a Jackson pickup.

ELECTRONICS

Guitar electronics can range from the very simple single humbucker, single volume knob approach championed by Eddie Van Halen on his infamous "Frankenstein" guitar to the marvelously complex controls and active preamps on a 1970s B.C. Rich Bich guitar. Most players and manufacturers choose something more moderate, with the two classic setups being that of the Fender Stratocaster and the Gibson Les Paul. Of course, many other options are available. Paul Reed Smith, Gibson, B.C. Rich, and others offer five-position rotary knobs, tone switches, phase inverters, coil taps, kill switches, active preamps, and more. We're going to explore the two classic setups first.

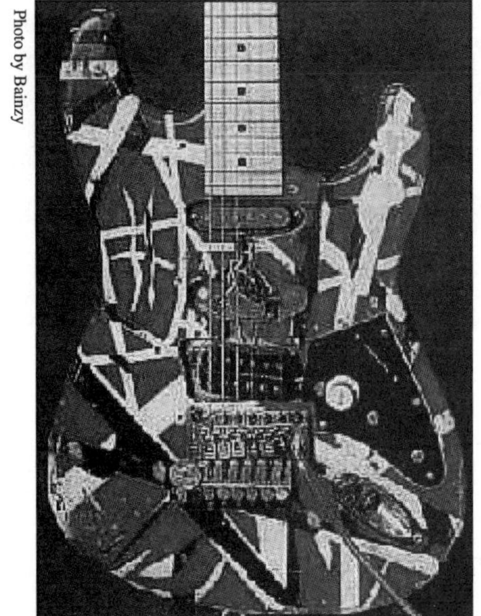

The Eddie Van Halen "Frankenstein" guitar has minimal electronics.

The Tom Delonge Signature ES-335 has minimal electronics.

Jerry Garcia "Rosebud" guitar with complex electronics.

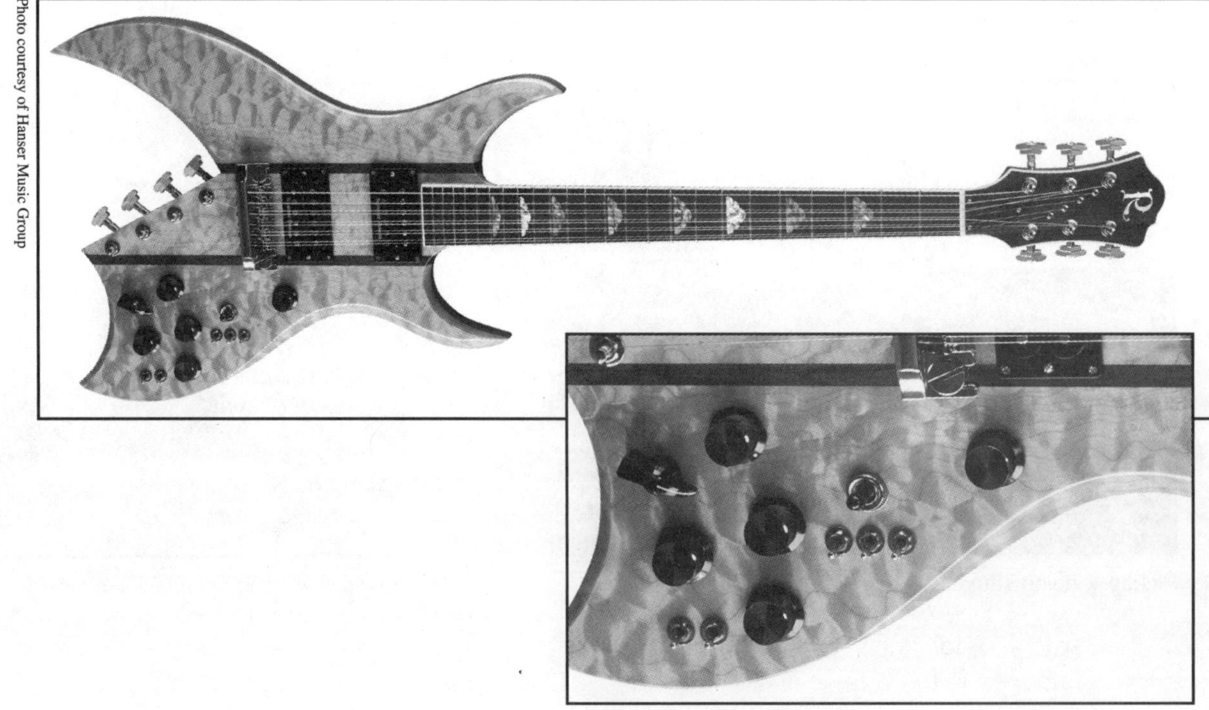

B.C. Rich Bich 10-string guitar features two active-boost circuits with individual controls.

Fender Stratocaster Setup

The classic Stratocaster features a versatile and intelligent electronic design with a layout that allows for quite a few tonal variations. For one thing, the single-coil pickups can be combined in adjacent pairs to create a humbucking-type sound. The resulting sound from combining the single-coils isn't quite as beefy as a real humbucker, but the hum is definitely eliminated! By flipping the pickup selector switch to the setting closest to the ground, you activate the bridge pickup to get the brashest sound available. There are countless subtle variations available with different pickup, tone knob, and volume knob combinations.

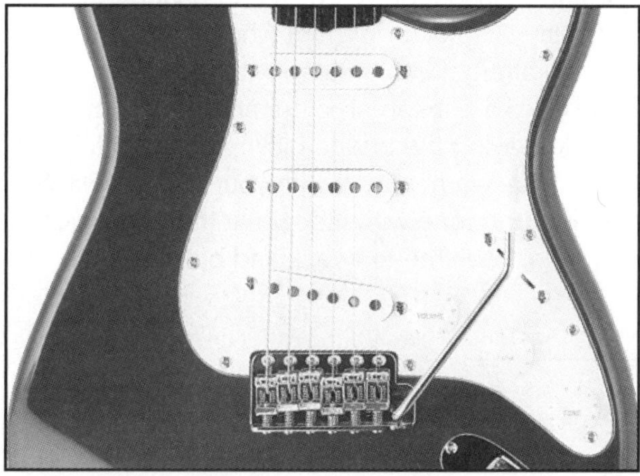

The classic Fender Stratocaster features three single-coil pickups, a five-position blade switch, one volume, and two tone controls.

Stratocaster Blade Switch Function

Position 1: (all the way up) Neck pickup only

Position 2: Combines neck and middle pickups

Position 3: Middle pickup only

Position 4: Combines middle and bridge pickups

Position 5: Bridge pickup only

Knob Functions

Volume: Works on all pickups and combinations.

Tone 1: Works on neck pickup only

Tone 2: Works on middle pickup only

The Strat has evolved to include many new and improved options over the years. It all began with the trend towards so-called "Superstrats," which were modified Strats that featured a humbucker in the bridge position. This was a major improvement because it allowed the Strat to enter sonic territory previously reserved for Gibson and its imitators.

Today, an American-made Deluxe Fender Stratocaster features powerful and improved controls. It looks exactly like the classic Strat layout, which is part of the charm. On today's Deluxe Strat, the pickups are all noiseless—so quiet their performance rivals that of traditional humbuckers. Also, there is an additional pickup concealed under the pickguard, which is activated by pressing a button in the volume knob. When engaged, it turns any of the five positions into a true humbucker!

Gibson Les Paul Setup

The Gibson Les Paul features an equally intelligent and versatile set of controls that are completely different from the Fender Strat. The Gibson features two humbucking pickups and a three-way toggle switch that selects either one pickup or combines both. Each pickup has its own dedicated volume and tone control. The creamy, warm neck pickup, the airy and harmonically rich middle position, and the aggressive bridge position humbucker all provide solid and usable sounds.

The Les Paul's simple three-way toggle switch configuration allows for a type of channel-switching function onboard the guitar. This is particularly useful for players who favor the "straight amping" approach where a guitar is plugged straight into an amp with no pedals or additional effects. To achieve channel-switching onboard a Gibson-style guitar, simply turn the volume and tone down a bit on the neck pickup while leaving the bridge pickup controls full up. With a little gain dialed in on the amp, you'll have a clean, warm sound with your toggle switch at the neck pickup position and a louder, brighter distorted tone with it down at the bridge position. In the middle, you'll split the difference in tone. Feel free to tweak and balance the contrast on the two pickups to your liking.

Photo courtesy of Gibson USA

Gibson Les Paul Standard.

A variation on the channel-switching idea is the "kill-switch" effect, which has been used by Tom Morello, Buckethead, Randy Rhoads, and others. To get this effect, simply turn the volume and tone controls all the way down on one of the pickups while leaving the controls for the other pickup full up—this way, your toggle switch will function as a kill switch. Toggling back and forth between pickups will result in an on-and-off sound. This is very useful with distortion. Try it!

Series and Parallel Pickup Wiring

A humbucking pickup can be wired in *series* or *parallel.* Typically, pickup wiring is done in series, which means the output of one coil is run through the other, and a single output is created by combining the outputs of both coils. In parallel wiring, each coil of the humbucker has a separate output which is combined later in the circuit. The sound is a little fatter with series wiring, which is why guitars often come this way from the factory.

Single-coil pickups are usually wired parallel, but in series wiring, the resulting sound has a humbucking quality. It doesn't sound exactly like a true humbucker, because the coils aren't right next to each other, but the combined pickups buck the hum even if they lack the muscle of a real humbucker. When positions 2 or 4 of the five-position blade switch are activated on a Strat, parallel wiring of single-coil pickups is engaged (unless they are wired to achieve something different). Those settings buck the hum but create a "quacky" sound due to the fact that pairs of adjacent pickups are *out of phase* with one another. Sound waves that are in phase with each other have peaks and valleys that are perfectly aligned so that the sound is strengthened. Out of phase waves are unsynchronized so that the peaks and valleys don't line up. If two waves are exactly out of phase they may cancel each other out, completely silencing the wave. This phenomenon is called *phase cancellation.* The waves of two adjacent pickups are partially out of phase and when combined create an interesting and desirable tone. Eric Clapton and other players of older Strats with three-position blade switches used to wedge the blade halfway between positions to get this sound.

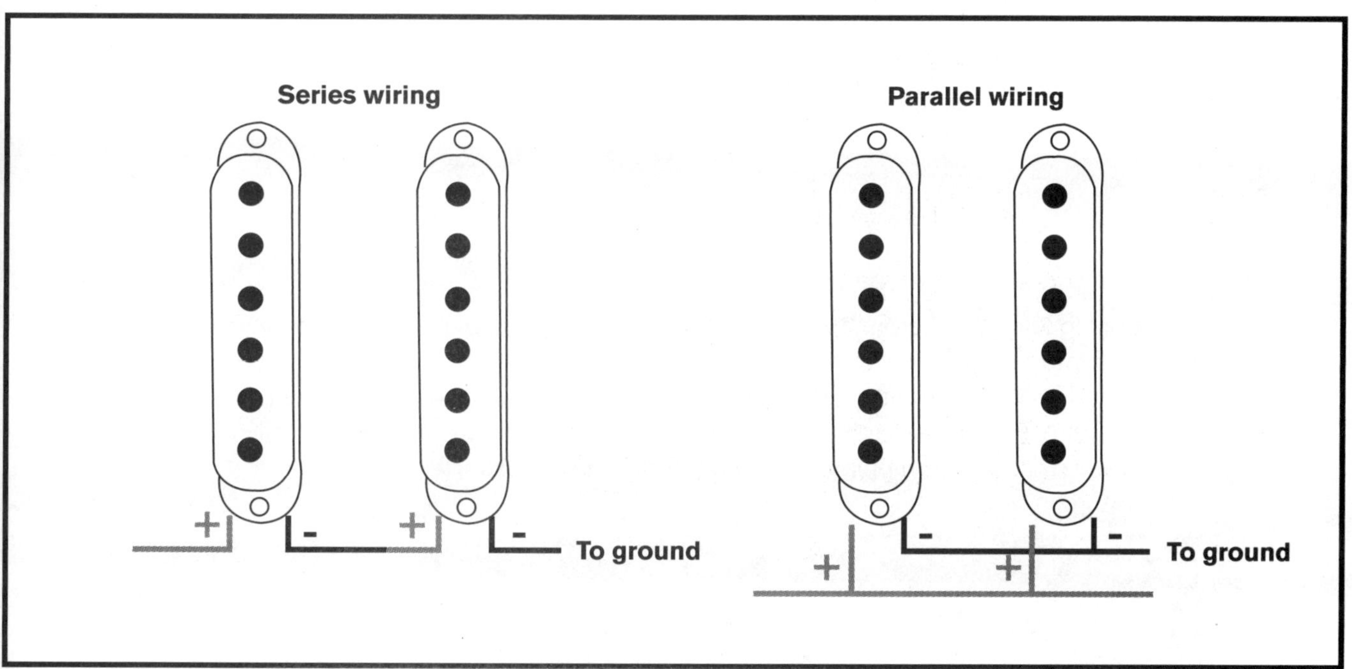

Series and parallel wiring of single-coil pickups.

Coil Tapping and Splitting

Coil *splitting* is often mistakenly referred to as coil *tapping.* Coil splitting disengages one of the two pickups inside a humbucker so that it sounds like a single coil. It is often activated by a push-pull potentiometer (that is doubling as the volume or tone knob) or via a simple mini toggle switch. This is a common modification that will come stock on many guitars. As Strat players load their guitars with humbuckers and add kill switches to make them more versatile, Les Paul players will add coil splitting to get closer to the clean Strat tones.

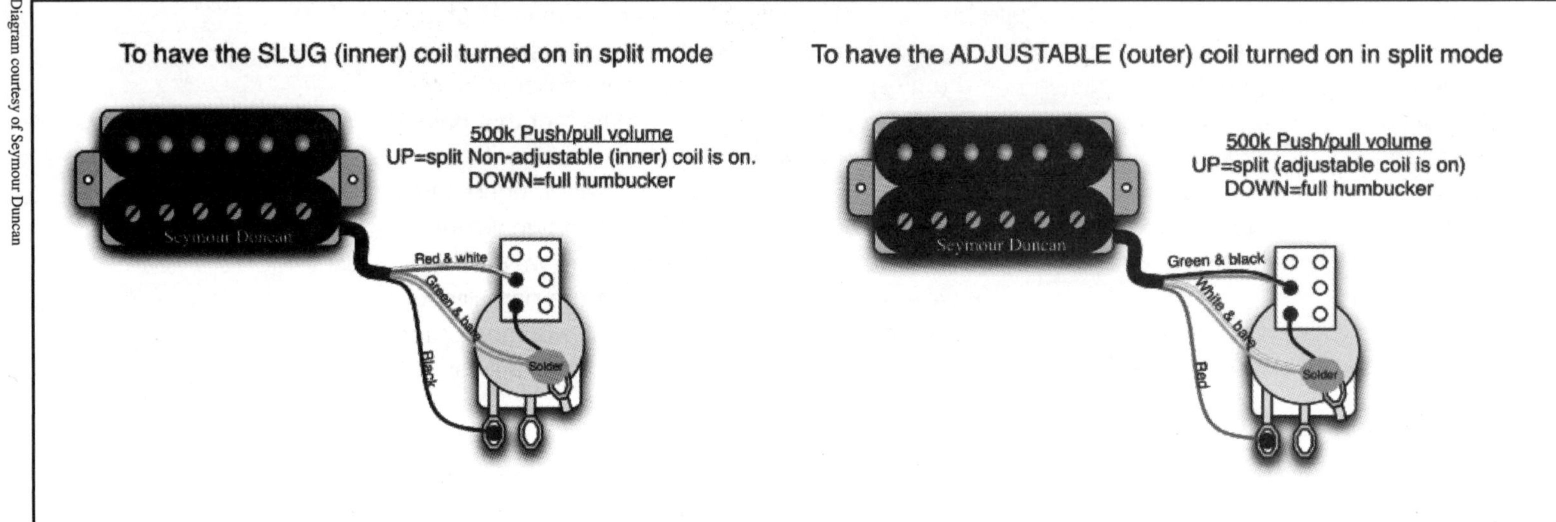

Seymour Duncan coil splitting diagram.

Coil tapping is quite different. Here, a portion of a single-coil pickup, often the bridge position, is tapped into to slightly color the overall sound, making it quieter, clearer, yet purely Stratty in a good way. Switching from the tapped pickup to the full-on one with a little gain on the amp can take you from crystal clean to mean in a heartbeat! This cool procedure is mostly overlooked; people who refer to coil tapping are often talking about coil splitting.

Custom staggered SSL-5 with tapped version available for dual output levels.

In and Out of Phase

A phase-inverting toggle switch can deliver more options as you combine pickups. When two wave forms are synchronized, so that the peak of each wave reaches the same amplitude at the same time, the waves are in phase. (For an explanation of "amplitude," see page 82.) If the opposite is the case, so that the valley of one wave happens just when the other wave is peaking, then they are out of phase. Waves that are in phase get twice as loud and ones that are exactly out of phase cancel each other out completely, resulting in total silence.

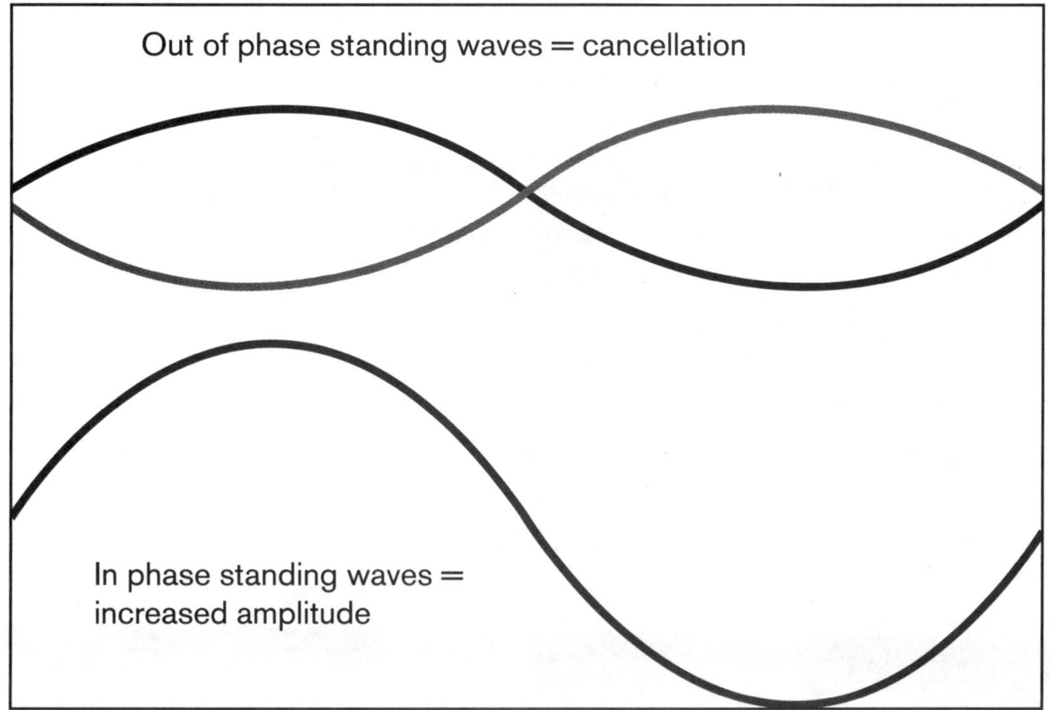

In and out of phase.

If a phase toggle switch is wired into a single-coil pickup, you will hear no difference at all when the switch is engaged, unless there is another pickup being used at the same time. When there are two pickups, the engagement of the switch changes the interaction of the waves being generated by the two pickups from being in phase, which creates a louder sound, to being out of phase, which partially cancels the signals so that certain frequencies are eliminated. A weaker, "quacky" sound results. Total phase cancellation doesn't occur when the switch is engaged because the pickups are not exact duplicates and are mounted in different locations. Therefore, they don't create identical waves or exhibit complete phase cancellation.

Kill Switches

A fairly common electronic modification is the addition of a kill switch to a Strat-style guitar or any guitar that can't get the same effect with stock electronics. Tom Morello and Buckethead both did this mod but in completely different ways. The toggle switch used by Morello activates the guitar when the switch is thrown down, so that when he hammers down onto a note it pops on and both hands work in unison. This would be absolutely counterintuitive with the arcade-style push button switch used by Buckethead. The Buckethead switch kills the guitar signal when it is pushed down. Try to play a Rage Against the Machine lick with this type of switch, and you'll drive yourself crazy! Eddie Van Halen can be heard using a kill switch at the end of his solo on "You Really Got Me" from Van Halen's debut, and Randy Rhoads can be heard using one on the rhythm guitar part to "I Don't Know" from *Blizzard of Ozz.*

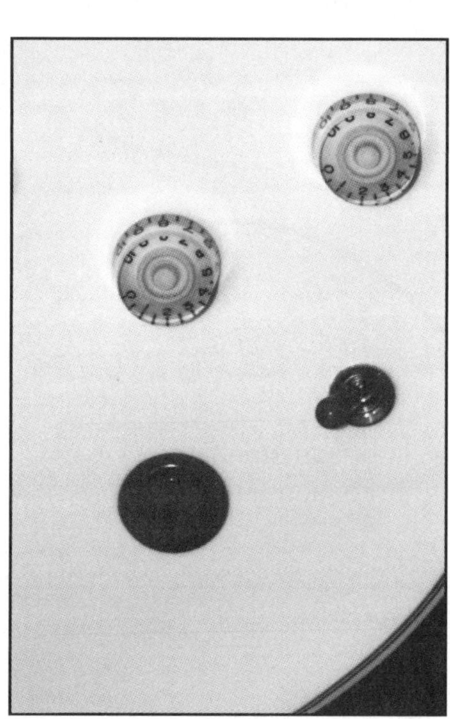
Close-up of push-button kill switch.

Photos by Alex Cotsaris

The Buckethead signature model Les Paul features two large, red push-button kill switches.

TONE WOODS

A tone wood is a wood that produces an actual pitch when a block of it is properly dried and then struck with an object such as a small mallet or drumstick. Plywood doesn't really qualify because the grains running in different directions hamper the natural resonance of the wood. That's why it's always best to choose an acoustic guitar made with as much solid wood as possible, especially the top. If the top isn't made of solid wood, it can't resonate well enough to project the best quality tone.

Acoustic Note: The wood on an acoustic guitar is much more important to tone than it is on an electric guitar, because the acoustic guitar must stand alone without electronics or amplification. The sound of an acoustic guitar depends wholly on wood, strings, craftsmanship, and design. Even so, the importance of wood quality has been questioned by some notable luthiers. The "Pallet Guitar," from Taylor Guitars, makes a case for the importance of design and craftsmanship over the use of fancy tone woods. Taylor recycled wood from actual shipping pallets to make 25 limited edition guitars. The guitars sound remarkably good and play easily! Of course, they probably would have sounded better if they had been made from fine tone woods, but the point is made: even on an acoustic guitar, tone wood isn't the be all and end all.

Taylor "Pallet Guitar."

Plywood in Electric Guitars

In electric guitar construction, tone wood is less important than in acoustic guitar construction. This is because electric guitar tone comes mainly from the pickups and strings. Many solid-body electrics will feature plywood bodies that are sanded down and painted brightly. These guitars are played on stages worldwide without having noticeably inferior tone. Expensive and highly regarded archtops, like the Gibson ES-335, also have plywood tops.

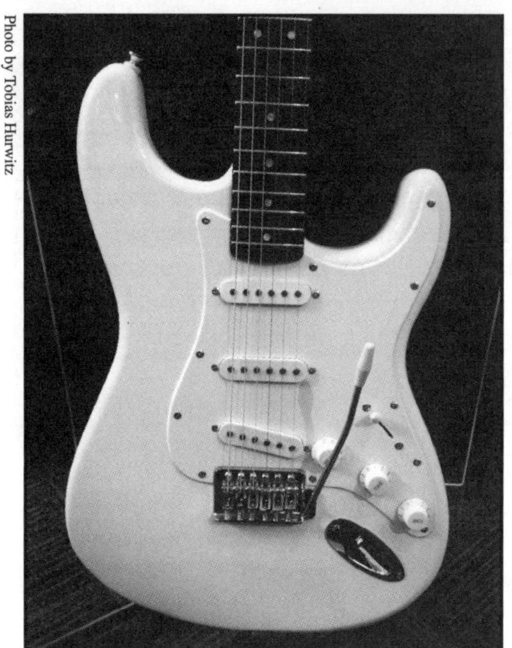

Cheap plywood-body electric guitar
(Fender Squier).

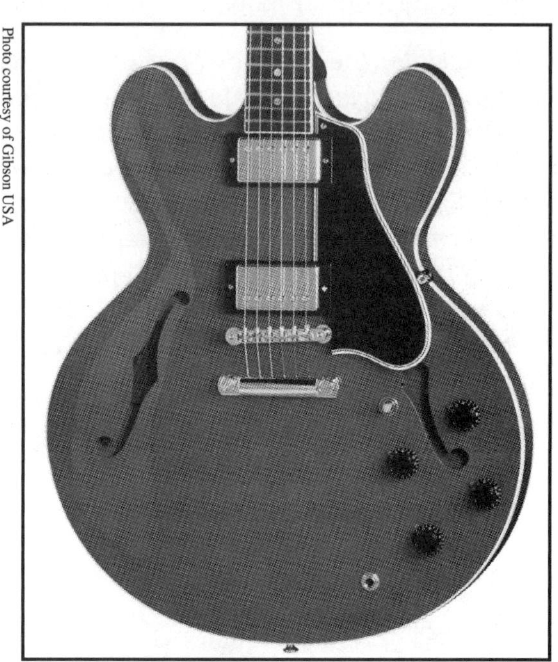

Expensive plywood-top electric guitar
(Gibson ES-335).

The luthier who is concerned with creating a high-quality instrument, not just a cheap one, will try to build an electric guitar that sounds as good as possible unplugged. The theory is if it sounds good unplugged, then it'll sound even better plugged in, which is probably true. Tone woods do sound better than plywood, and it does, in fact, make a difference. The neck and body both affect the sound, and these can be made with single-wood or multi-wood construction. Tone woods sound, look, and feel different from each other, and some are endangered species, making them extremely difficult to obtain. Luthiers have been known to "harvest" antique desks to get their hands on small quantities of guitar-grade Brazilian rosewood—a highly desirable tone wood. Many consumers just want to see a stunning flamed maple top peeking through a translucent finish on their guitar, and some like the smooth tight-grained feel of an ebony fretboard under their fingers. These, and many other factors, come into play when building or choosing a guitar.

Let's have a look at a few guitars and the woods used to construct them.

Wood Setup for Gibson SG Standard

Body: Mahogany

Neck: Mahogany

Fretboard: Indian Rosewood

Gibson SG Standard.

Mahogany

The Les Paul Special, Les Paul Jr., and the SG all have bodies and necks made from mahogany, which has a warm, dark tone with a pleasant but subdued high end, along with good sustain, grit, and character. The color of mahogany is medium to dark brown with a cross grain that makes it a very stable wood. It comes mainly from Africa and Central America, and is often combined with other fine tone woods, such as maple, to form multi-wood bodies like those on the Paul Reed Smith Custom 24 and Gibson Les Paul.

Indian Rosewood

Indian rosewood is the most commonly used wood for modern fretboard construction in electric guitars. The color is a darker brown than mahogany, and the grain is somewhat loose, imparting a feeling of slight grit or resistance when bending or sliding, unlike the smoother feel of maple, ebony, and Brazilian rosewood fretboards. The tone is dark as well. Leo Fender introduced rosewood fingerboards as a substitution for maple ones in 1959. Fender had teetered back and forth as to which to use over the years until both were finally offered as options.

Brazilian Rosewood

Brazilian rosewood is a rare and endangered wood. It's heavier than Indian rosewood and offers superior tone and smoother feel. Brazilian rosewood is used for many purposes including the back and sides of acoustic guitars, necks, fretboards, and more.

Wood Setup for Paul Reed Smith Custom 24

Body: Mahogany with carved flame maple top

Neck: Mahogany

Fretboard: Indian Rosewood

Wood Setup for Paul Reed Smith Custom 24.

Maple

There are several varieties of maple, each with lovely but differing grain patterns. The flamed, quilted, and bird's eye varieties of maple are often seen shining through translucent or sunburst finishes on guitars with carved tops. This creates not only a stunning visual effect, but an enhancement in tone and comfort. Maple is lighter in weight and brighter in tone than mahogany, so when a carved maple top is attached to a mahogany body, the finished guitar is lighter, better sounding, and fancier looking.

Maple is also used for fingerboards and guitar necks. Maple fingerboards are smooth and produce snappy, bright tones.

Wood Setup for Fender Stratocaster

Body: Swamp Ash

Neck: Maple

Fingerboard: Maple

Wood Setup for Fender Stratocaster.

Swamp Ash

The bodies of classic 1950s-era Fender guitars were made of swamp ash, a wood that is still commonly used for the bodies of fine guitars. This dark-blond wood looks great under a translucent finish and is known for its sweet twang. Guitar-grade swamp ash must be taken from the lower part of the tree, which is often submerged in water. It grows in the wetlands of the southern United States and is light and resonant. Northern ash is harder and offers more brightness but isn't generally preferred over swamp ash, which is considered the best ash for guitar building.

Wood Setup for Carvin Custom 7-String

Body: Koa

Neck: Koa with maple stripes

Fingerboard: Ebony

Wood Setup for Carvin Custom 7-String.

Koa

Koa is an exotic reddish-brown wood that is only found in the Hawaiian Islands. Though fast growing, Koa is a protected wood so it isn't used much for mass-produced guitars. It is more likely to be found in limited editions and as an option when custom ordering a high-end guitar. Koa delivers a warm, balanced tone with a distinctive upper midrange.

Ebony

Ebony is the hardest wood available for guitar construction and is very expensive and desirable. The grain is very tight, making it almost invisible, and the surface is smooth, which is an ideal match for fast playing when used as a fretboard wood. The hardness of the wood makes for a durable fretboard, less susceptible to denting and firmly holding the frets in place. The tone is clear and bright with nice string attack, and the dark, black color makes it visually attractive.

More About Guitar-Building Materials

Dozens of types of woods, exotic and otherwise, have been used in guitar construction, but synthetic materials, such as Plexiglass, resin, and metal, have been used as well. The choices are many and the materials used will affect tone, feel, and appearance.

The words used to describe the sonic properties of wood are subjective at best. Who can say exactly what gritty, full, resonant, brilliant, snappy, murky, chimey, or balanced really means in terms of the subtle differences heard in the resonant frequencies of planks or chunks of lumber? Even wood cut from the same tree, then dried or finished differently, will sound different. The understanding of tone woods is a deep and complex topic that will forever spark innovation and debate among luthiers and guitar enthusiasts. Hopefully, this brief discussion has helped clarify some of the varieties and variables available for consideration.

THE TRUSS ROD

The *truss rod* is a metal rod that runs inside the guitar neck in a routed groove under the fretboard. The rod may be installed so that the adjustment end can be accessed either at the headstock or through the body. Truss rod adjustments made through the body on acoustic guitars require you to reach inside the sound hole with an Allen wrench, which isn't too bad, but on solid-body electrics with bolt-on necks, the neck will need to be removed to access the rod. Truss rod adjustments are much easier to deal with when they are done at the headstock end. This should be considered when choosing a guitar.

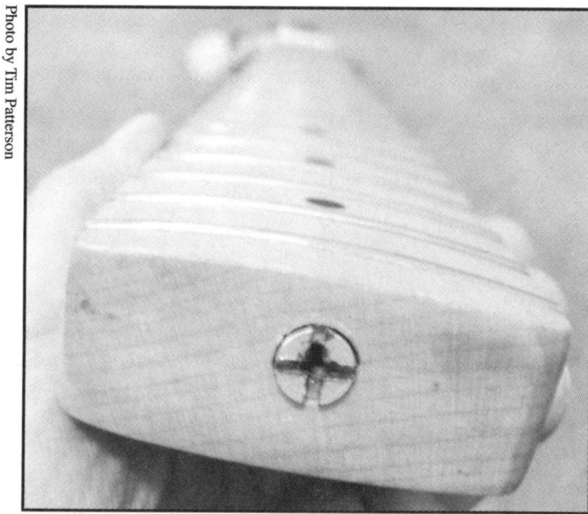

Truss rod, front view.

Truss rod tension controls the straightness of the guitar neck. Tightening it raises the neck closer to the strings, while loosening it lowers the neck away from the strings. If a neck has a problem such as a bump in the middle, causing the strings to buzz, or a dip that causes uncomfortably high action, a simple half-turn adjustment can remedy the problem in a flash. The rod should always be adjusted with the strings on and tuned to whatever tuning the player uses the most. This is because the truss rod counters the tension of the strings and different tunings and string gauges will mean different truss rod settings.

Most professionals adjust their truss rods fairly frequently. Setting up a guitar to function properly in a drop tuning or with a different string gauge usually requires tweaking the truss rod. Sometimes, the action of a guitar can shift overnight, causing a buzz or bad action. These conditions are also cause for an adjustment.

When turning a truss rod, one shouldn't crank the rod. Just turn it a quarter or half turn, and then look down the neck to see the effect it's having in real time. You can turn it some more if you need to, but remember that 95% of the change in the neck will occur within a minute or two of turning the rod. If you don't like the results, you can always turn the rod back to the previous setting and the guitar will return to normal.

FRETBOARD RADIUS

Though the fretboard of a guitar may appear flat at first glance, it is actually curved. This curvature, measured at the nut, is called the *fretboard radius.* Manufacturers describe fretboard radius as a measurement in inches. The smaller the measurement, which represents the size of the circle, the greater the curvature of the fretboard. This may seem counterintuitive, but understand that the measurement refers to the radius of a circle. See the diagram below for a clearer representation of the concept.

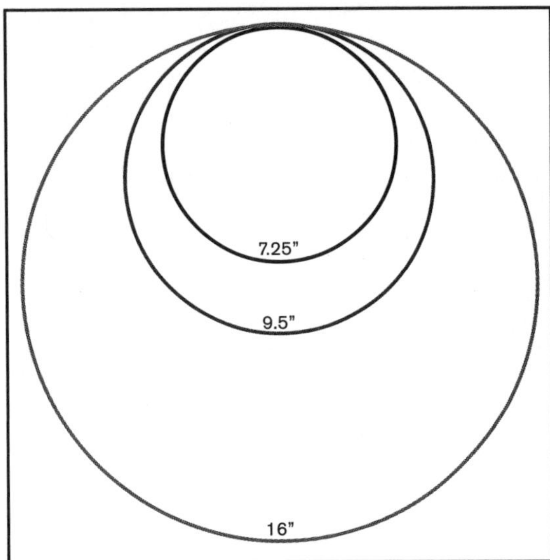

The larger the circle, the flatter the fretboard.

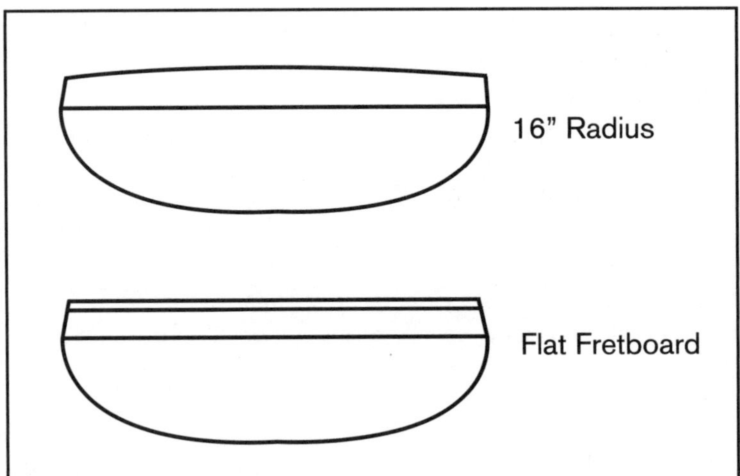

The 16" radius is typical of a Jackson-style guitar whereas the flat fretboard is found on a nylon-string classical guitar.

How Radius Affects Playability and Performance

Rhythm guitarists tend to like guitars with more curvature in the fretboard because it makes playing barre chords and chord-melodies easier. The downside to more curvature is it makes bending notes and playing scales slightly more difficult. For this reason, lead guitarists and sweep pickers tend to choose guitars with flatter fretboards. There are certainly exceptions to this trend, and the difference in playability is subtle enough that most of us can easily switch from a vintage Stratocaster, with a highly curved fretboard, to a classical guitar, with a perfectly flat one, with little or no difficulty.

Compound or Conical Fretboard Radius

Some luthiers have attempted to create a best-of-both-worlds scenario by crafting fretboards with a diminishing radius. The lower part is curved more to make rhythm playing easier, while the high part is flatter to facilitate bending and scale runs. The radius for these guitars changes smoothly since it is modeled on a cone, not a circle. The diagrams below illustrate this concept.

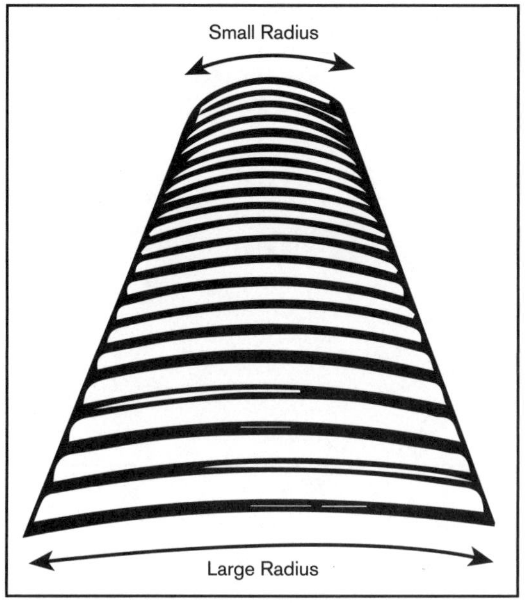

Compound radius fretboard. The higher frets are less curved than the lower frets.

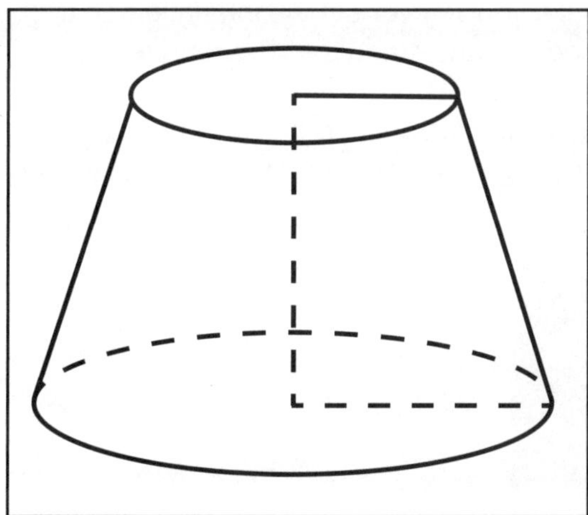

The cone model helps the luthier achieve a smooth radius change because the circles evenly diminish in size as they rise up the cone.

The following chart shows the fretboard radius of various guitars.

Guitar Neck Radius Guide

GUITAR	RADIUS
Classical Guitar	Flat
Vintage Fender Strat	7.25"
Modern Fender Strat	9.5"
PRS Custom 24	11.5"
Guitars with Original Floyd Rose Locking Nut	10"
Gibson Guitars	10" to 12"
Ibanez Guitars	12"
Jackson Guitars	16"

SCALE LENGTH

Scale length is the length of the guitar string from the nut to the bridge—the vibrating portion of the string. It's calculated by measuring from the edge of the nut, where it meets the fretboard, to the center of the 12th fret and then doubling that distance.

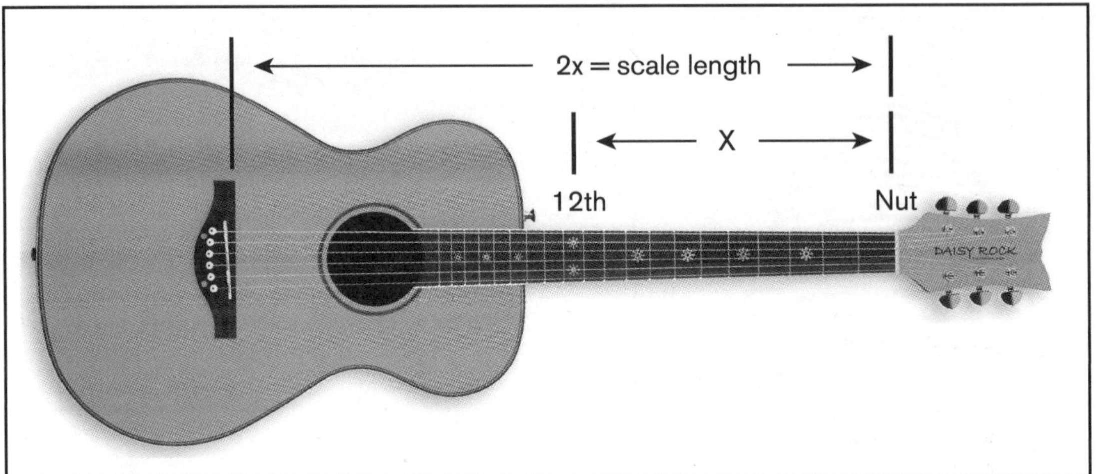

Scale length.

The reason it is not simply calculated by measuring from the nut to the bridge is because bridges and bridge saddles are almost always set at an angle to achieve proper intonation. This variation of string length is called *compensation.* If you've ever set the intonation on a guitar with an adjustable bridge you may have noticed that the string saddles tend to line up in angled rows of three saddles. This pattern is common to all makes and models of electric guitars with adjustable bridge saddles, but the angle makes measuring from nut to bridge iffy at best, so that's why it's best to determine scale length by measuring from the nut to the center of the 12th fret and then doubling.

Photo by Tobias Hurwitz

Note the two angled rows of saddles on this properly adjusted bridge.

Conventional Scale Lengths

Many guitars are modeled after the scale length of Fender Stratocasters and Telecasters, which is 25.5". Gibson and Gibson-style guitars tend to feature a shorter scale length of 24.75" with slight variations. Paul Reed Smith guitars fall just between the two at an even 25". This small difference in length of only 0.75" or so can substantially affect the tone and feel of guitars.

The two most-immediately tangible qualities affected by scale length are string tension and harmonic response. The slightly shorter scale length of a Gibson-style guitar produces less string tension, which makes bending strings and pressing down a bit easier than it would be on the longer Fender guitars. Also, the shorter scale produces a warmer tone but lacks the crisp response and bell-like chime of the Fender. Which is better? Well, that's up to the player and there are many who prefer the PRS scale length, which splits the difference. Any guitar can have reduced string tension and a warmer tone just by tuning it down, as Jimi Hendrix did with his Strat. Using heavy strings, like Stevie Ray Vaughan did, can make up for the reduced string tension on a down-tuned guitar. These and other options provide many possible avenues for tone geeks to explore on their endless quest for that magic combination of great tone and playability.

Acoustic Note: *It's easy to imagine that the difference in playability between acoustic and electric guitars is entirely due to the lighter strings that electrics tend to be strung with. Electric guitars commonly come new from the factory strung with .009 light-gauge strings while acoustics come with .011s. This makes a big difference, but so does the fact that acoustics usually have a slightly longer scale length. The chart below shows the scale lengths of a few electric guitars for reference and comparison.*

Scale Length Guide

GUITAR	SCALE LENGTH
Fender Stratocaster	25.5"
Fender Telecaster	25.5"
PRS Custom 24	25"
PRS Custom 22	25"
Rickenbacker Model 330	24.75"
Gibson Les Paul Standard	24.75"
Gibson SG Standard	24.75"
Fender Jaguar	24"
Fender Mustang	22"

FRETS

There are many things to consider about frets, the first and foremost being their height. After a few years of playing—the amount of time will vary from player to player–fret wires can become worn down and dinged. Intonation and playability can start to go downhill. These are signs your frets need maintenance work.

Fret Maintenance

When you play a guitar with new frets and notice passages that you have been having difficulty with are now suddenly easier, or chord voicings with questionable intonation on your guitar now ring true, then you should realize your guitar is overdue for a fret *leveling* and *dressing.* Leveling and dressing the frets is the process of filing and sanding the frets smooth so they perform like new, though they will be a little lower in height. Edging work may also be needed if the fretboard has dried out and shrunken so that the frets stick out over the side. These procedures should be done by a trained professional. A guitar can usually handle five to ten levelings before requiring a complete re-fretting (completely replacing the frets). The taller and wider the frets, the more levelings they can withstand. If your guitar has gone too long between levelings, then a fewer number of levelings will be possible. Replacing the frets is a fairly expensive job, but it will really bring your instrument back to life.

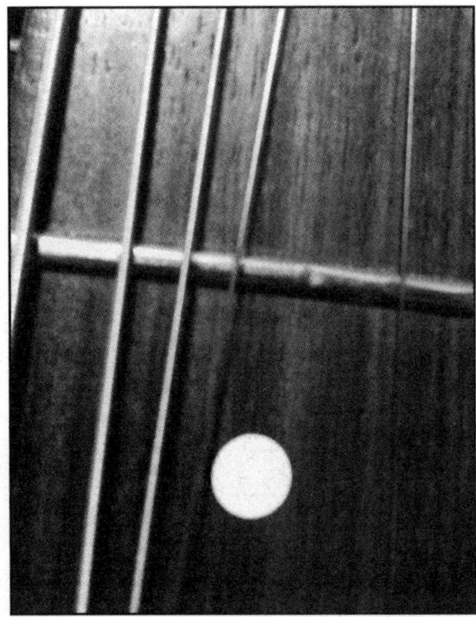

Worn fret in need of leveling and dressing.

Fret Type and Size

The fret wire is attached to the fretboard via a square metal tang which is hidden from view under the *crown*, or top, of the fret (see illustration to the right). The width and height of the crown are both important considerations. Since the fret location defines a note's exact pitch, the thinner the width of the crown the better the intonation. But, thinner frets will also wear out faster. Taller, wider frets are generally preferred by string benders and shredders, because they reduce resistance against the fretboard to make it easier to play fast technical music. The drawback with tall, wide frets is too much finger pressure can cause the strings to go sharp. At first, this may seem like a major issue, but it might be best to learn to adapt from the higher pressure required to play a steel-string acoustic guitar, without buzzing, to the feathery light touch required for electric guitars with light strings and jumbo frets.

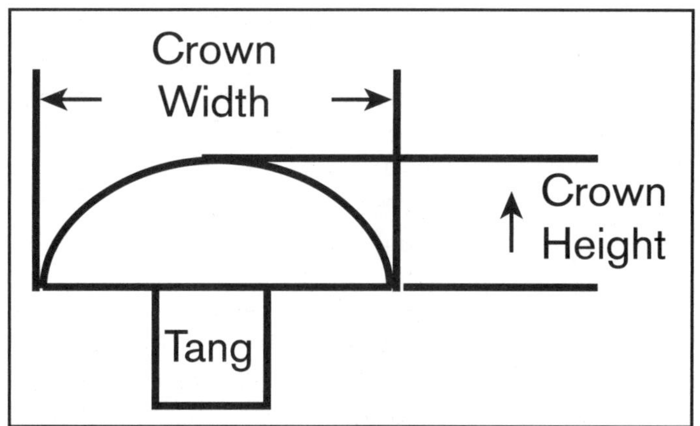

Illustration of fret.

Fret wires are made from a variety of metals, including nickel, soft nickel, brass, stainless steel, and nickel-free copper alloy. Each of these feature different hardnesses that will affect their durability and ease of maintenance for the luthier.

Number of Frets

Another important question to ask is how many frets do you need? Most electric guitars have 22, but the number of frets available on most standard models range from 21 to 24. Of course it's a matter of personal choice, but if your style of playing demands bending the D note at the 22nd fret of the 1st string up to E, then you might want a 24-fret instrument. If you play a lot at the high end of the guitar neck, then you might even consider something like the Ibanez Xiphos guitar, which has 27 frets.

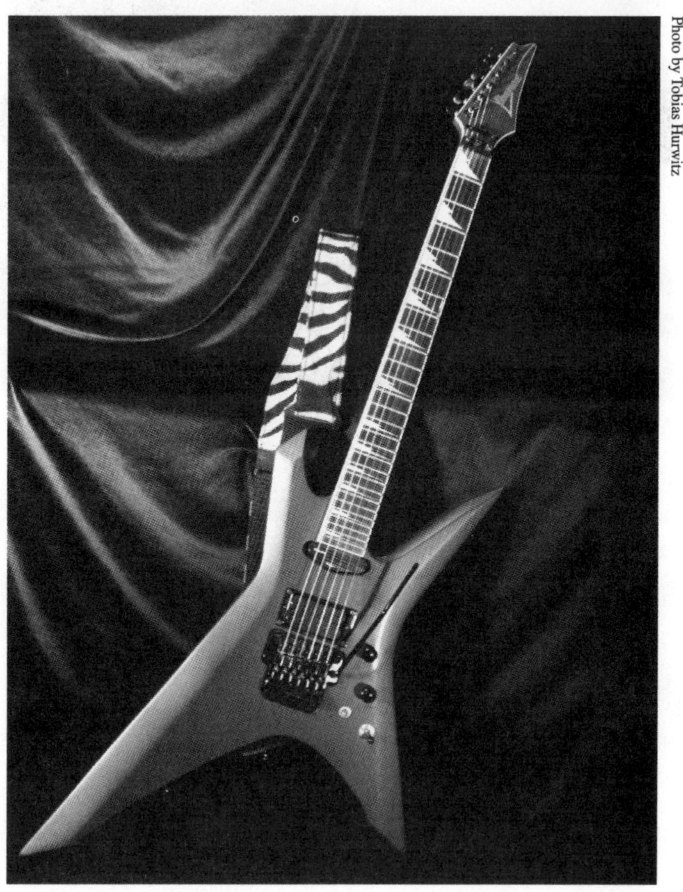

27-fret Ibanez Xiphos.

NECK PROFILE

The shape of the guitar neck affects the feel of a guitar in a prominent and immediately noticeable way. It should really be a make-or-break factor when selecting a new guitar. Playability and tone are always things to consider, but easier playability usually results in a weaker tone. A fatter neck produces more sustain and a fatter tone, but it's harder to do things like wrap your thumb around the top of the neck, like Jimi Hendrix, or stretch your fingers out really far like Eddie Van Halen. Technical players tend to prefer thinner necks with the "D" shape pictured below.

If you happen to own a few guitars, check to see if you can identify the neck profile of each and re-evaluate what you like and dislike about the feel and tone of each guitar. Next time you're in a music store, see if you can find a neck profile that feels really great. How's the tone? Can you fatten it up by tweaking the amp, or do you really just need a fatter neck? Most of us will go for playability, because if it doesn't feel good, then you're not likely to sound good either way.

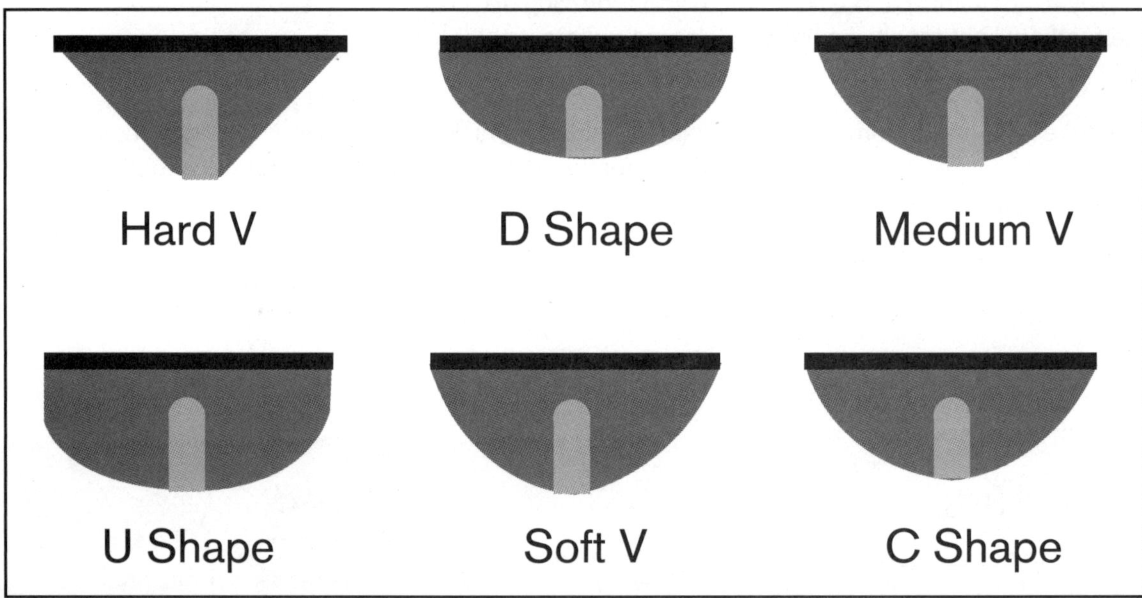

Neck profile chart.

TUNING PEGS (MACHINE HEADS)

Tuning pegs, or machine heads, on a guitar come in many varieties—from the violin-style wooden pegs used on old-school Spanish guitars to the modern mechanical tuners that turn by themselves via computer control on the Gibson Robot Guitar. The two major types of tuning pegs are standard and locking.

Standard pegs all have one thing in common: the string is attached to the post by winding it. In the case of vintage-style Fender tuning pegs, the string end is fed down into a hole in the tuning peg post, which secures it nicely for wrapping. Most other tuners have a hole cut through the post for the string to pass through before wrapping.

Vintage-style Fender tuner.

Standard Gibson-style tuner.

Locking tuners are mainly for use on guitars with whammy bars. Sperzel introduced locking tuners in 1983, and PRS popularized them in 1986. The idea behind locking tuners is the string locks directly onto the post with no wrapping needed, speeding up the stringing process and eliminating tuning problems. Many players choose to upgrade to locking tuners, whether or not a trem is installed.

Spurzel-style locking tuners made by Fender.

THE NUT

The nut is situated at the end of the fretboard, near the headstock. Its slots support and space the strings properly, holding them at the correct level so they don't buzz against the first few frets. If the nut is set too high, the guitar will have high action and poor intonation, while if it's set too low, there will be buzzing. Some nuts are made of metal, mostly on bass guitars, and feature screws that adjust the height of each string or the overall height of each side of the nut. This is a very useful feature for relieving fret buzz quickly and easily.

Photo by Ethan Prater

Height-adjustable nut on Warwick Thumb Bass.

Various materials have been used to construct the nut, including bone, wood, plastic, ivory, metal, and graphite. Plastics, graphite, and other non-slip materials are used on guitars with whammy bars to help alleviate tuning problems that result from strings getting stuck in the nut and not returning to their original positions after whammy use. This system, combined with a straight headstock and locking tuners, is used by Fender on its Deluxe American Stratocaster, PRS on its Custom 24, and by many other whammy-equipped guitars.

Photo by Tobias Hurwitz

PRS Custom 24 with super slippery synthetic nut.

The Locking Nut

The locking nut is another option for staying in tune while using the whammy bar, and it is usually found in conjunction with a Floyd Rose double-locking tremolo. The locking nut tightens each string individually, so even if a string breaks, the tension will not change between the nut and the tuner. Locking nuts do their job well but are somewhat inconvenient when it comes to changing strings and tuning, since an Allen wrench is required to make adjustments.

Ibanez JS Series with locking nut.

Roller nuts offer yet another solution to whammy-induced tuning problems.

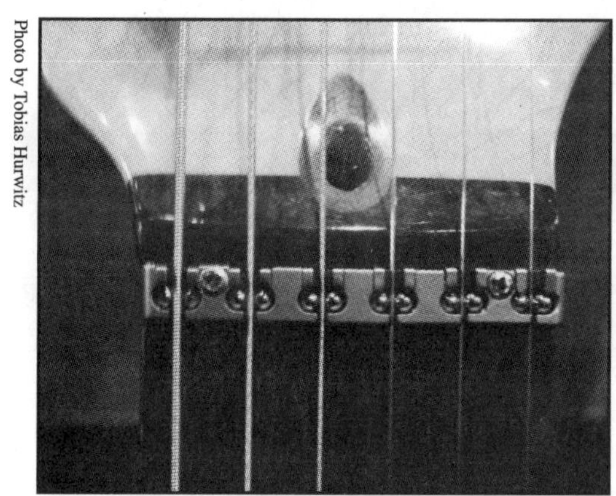

Roller nuts.

The signature Gibson Johnny A. model is equipped with a standard nut. Johnny himself lubricates the nut so that he can use a traditional Bigsby tremolo much more actively than one might expect and still stay in perfect tune. We'll cover the Bigsby tremolo on page 78.

Signature Gibson Johnny A. guitar.

The Compensated Nut

A *compensated nut* is designed to eliminate or improve tuning problems inherent with the guitar. A piano also has inherent tuning problems, but tempering helps spread the tuning issues out evenly over the range of the instrument, making them mostly unnoticeable. The compensated nut attempts to solve this problem. It features string notches in the nut that are cut slightly differently to allow for individual string length to be slightly shortened or lengthened according to the best judgment of a luthier or designer. This system certainly improves intonation and is especially popular on acoustic guitars whose bridges don't tend to be adjustable.

Compensated nut.

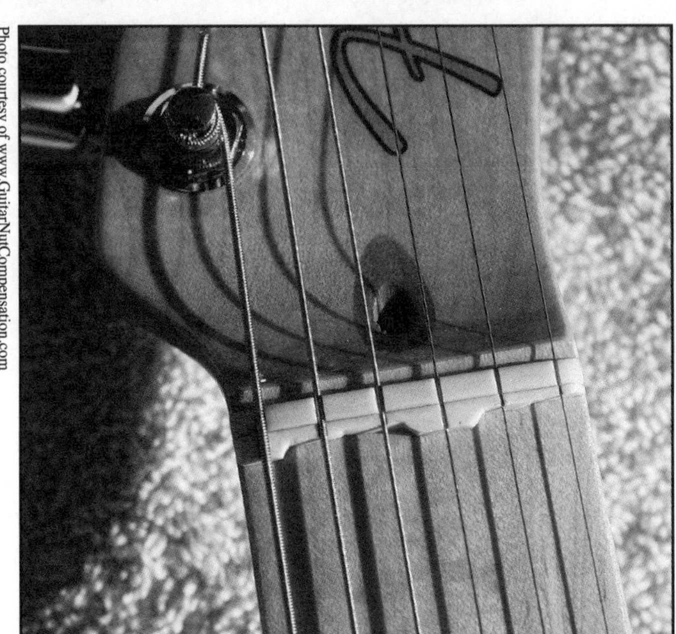

This is a custom compensated nut, which adjusts the ratio of the scale length versus the fretted length of each string. This allows "in tune" playing both at the lower open chords as well as the entire neck.

THE BRIDGE

Guitar strings make first contact with the body of the guitar at the bridge. The strings may be attached to the bridge or to a tailpiece located next to the bridge. Bridge styles include the simple, wooden Danelectro bridge; the fully adjustable, whammy-equipped Floyd Rose; and the ultramodern, automatically self-tuning EverTune bridge.

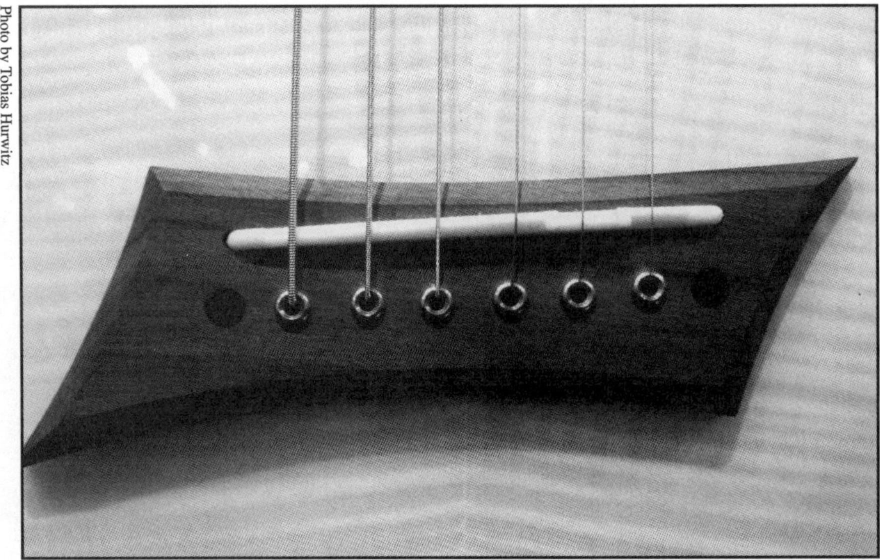

Simple bridge on Michael Kelly electric archtop.

The more adjustable a bridge is, the more control the guitarist will have over action and intonation. The Gibson Tune-o-matic is a good example of a highly adjustable bridge. It features individual string saddles that are adjustable up, down, forward, and backwards, and the overall bridge height is adjustable with two sturdy screws on each side.

The bridge must be properly set for a guitar to have good action and intonation. In some cases, there are fine tuners conveniently located on the bridge so that tuning can be done with the picking hand during performances.

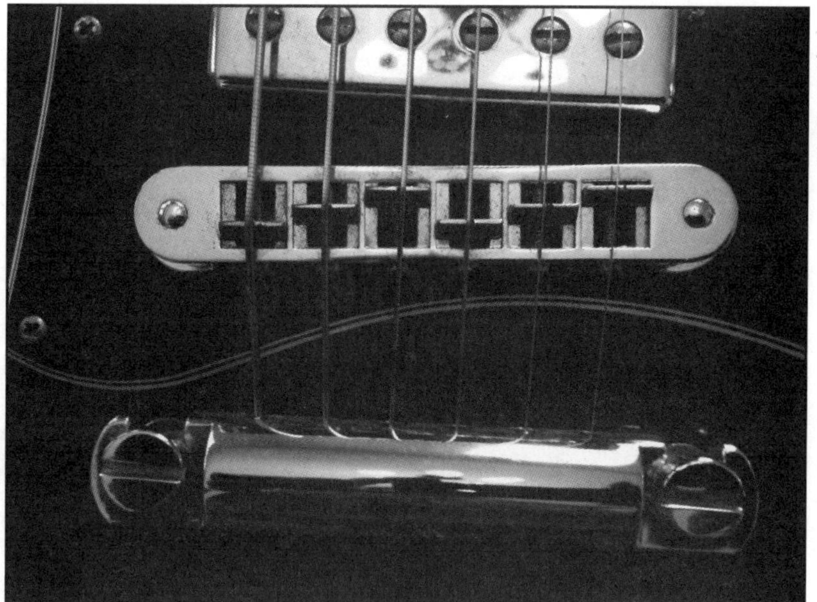

Gibson Tune-o-matic bridge.

One of the most notable modern innovations in bridge design is the EverTune bridge. This mechanical wonder maintains perfect tension and tuning for each string with an ingenious series of springs and levers concealed in the guitar's body. The EverTune system requires special routing for installation, and thin-bodied guitars, such as the Gibson SG, are not compatible with the system. The device keeps your guitar in perfect tune for the life of the strings, even with string bending!

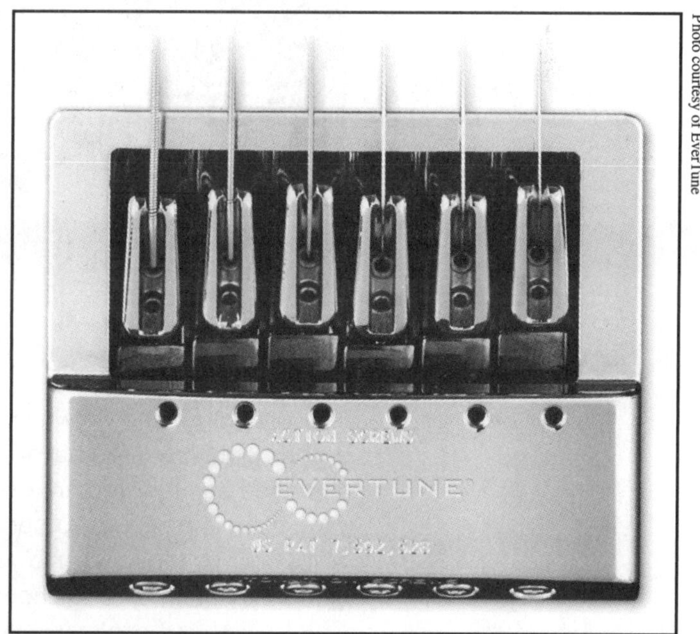

EverTune bridge.

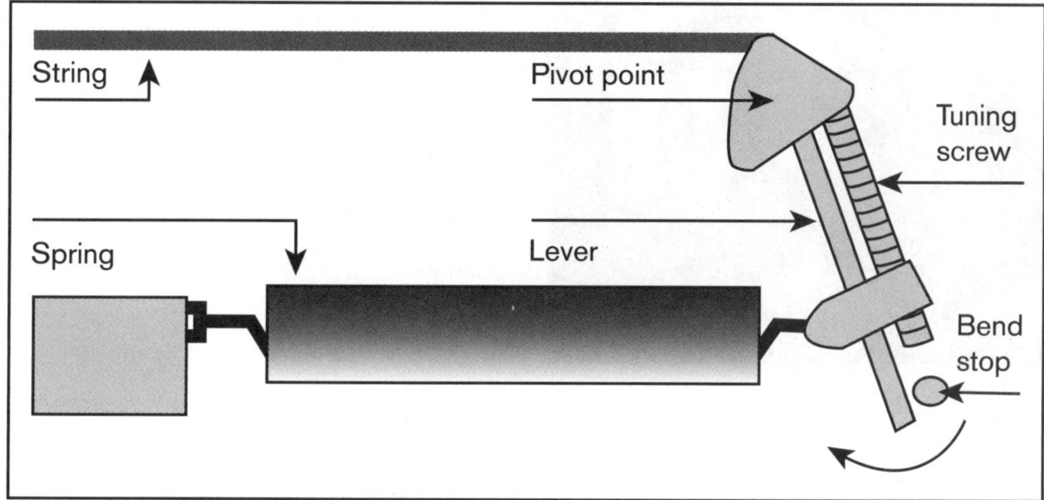

The mechanics behind the EverTune bridge.

THE WHAMMY BAR

The whammy bar raises or lowers the pitches of the strings, enabling a wide range of effects from gentle chord vibrato to full dive bombs, chirping sounds, siren wails, and more. The old-school Bigsby-style units mount to the top of the guitar without physical alterations, such as routing. Bigsbys are mainly used for gentle vibrato and slight dipping of the strings for which they function beautifully.

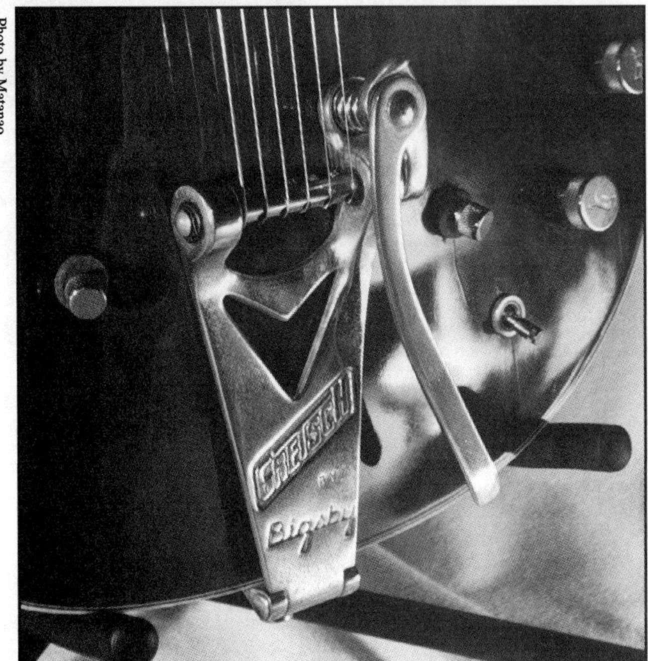

Bigsby whammy bar.

The vintage Strat-style whammy bar is capable of many wonders in the hands of the likes of Jimi Hendrix, but it wreaks havoc on tuning and is plagued with other problems. For instance, the threaded bar itself requires being screwed farther and farther in each time so that it becomes rare, if not impossible, to position in a consistently comfortable position. Vintage guitar purists still swear by these whammy bars, but those of us who simply want to play in comfort and with good intonation tend to choose more modern alternatives.

Vintage Fender whammy bar.

The Floyd Rose double-locking tremolo is probably the most popular whammy bar in production. There are definitely pros and cons to the Floyd Rose, but it undoubtedly feels good, stays in tune, and sounds exceptionally good.

The Floyd Rose features a double-locking system, which means the strings are attached directly to the bridge saddles, so that there is no room for slippage whatsoever. The ball end must be cut off before attaching the string and an Allen wrench is required. The other part of the double-locking system is the locking nut (see page 75), which will also require an Allen wrench. When both ends of the system are in place, your string will have no slippage at all. The Floyd Rose bar itself doesn't thread in and can be easily set to dangle freely or stay where you leave it. The bar is so solidly attached to the guitar that the whole weight of the guitar can be supported by the bar alone!

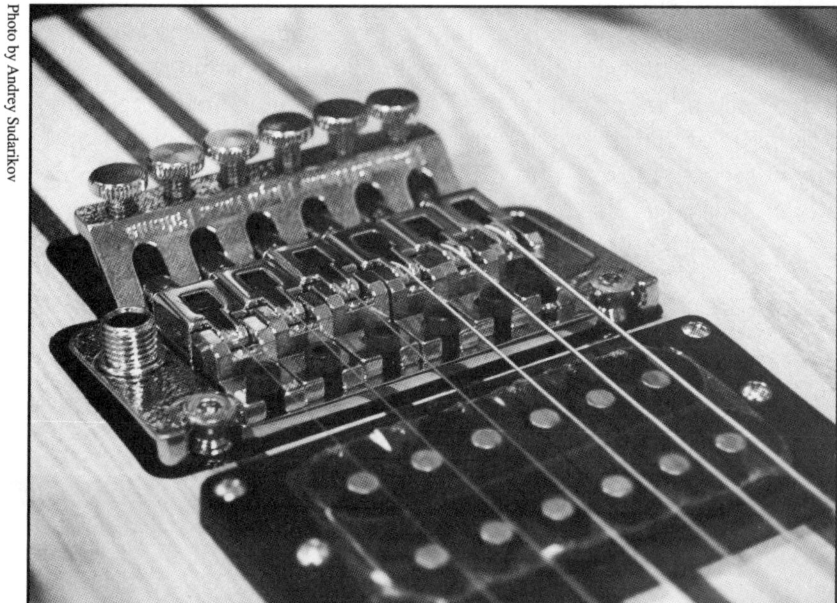

Photo by Andrey Sudarikov

Floyd Rose double-locking tremolo.

Most guitarists set their Floyd Rose to "float," which means the bar can move in either direction and is capable of tightening and loosening the strings. Once the strings are stretched and tuned, the Floyd Rose system works very well. One problem, though, is when you change the tension of one string it changes the tension of the rest of the strings, requiring you to have to tune the guitar several times. Also, the locking nut will need to be loosened with the wrench to tune it, and then re-tightened. The re-tightening causes the guitar to go slightly sharp, so that's where the fine tuners come into play. With this system, when a string breaks, the whole guitar goes out of tune.

How to Live in Peace with Your Double-Locking Trem

- Decide on one tuning for the guitar—set it up for that tuning, and leave it that way.

- Decide on one string gauge for the guitar—set it up for that gauge, and leave it that way.

- Stretch your strings thoroughly before tightening the nut.

- Never remove all of the strings at once.

- Replace strings one at a time, and tune each one to pitch before moving on to the next string.

Naturally, there are those of us who don't want to fool around with wrenches just to tune or restring a guitar. Enter the Paul Reed Smith–style floating trem to the rescue. Like the Floyd Rose, the PRS bar doesn't thread in, so it conveniently stays where you want it and maintains tuning extremely well. Strings don't slip at the bridge on the PRS trem, and the headstock and nut are designed to eliminate slippage at the other end—achieved through the use of locking tuners (see page 73), a slippery nut (see page 74), and a straight string pull to the pegs. Fender and other manufacturers also offer similar PRS-style setups. This type of whammy-bar system has become very popular.

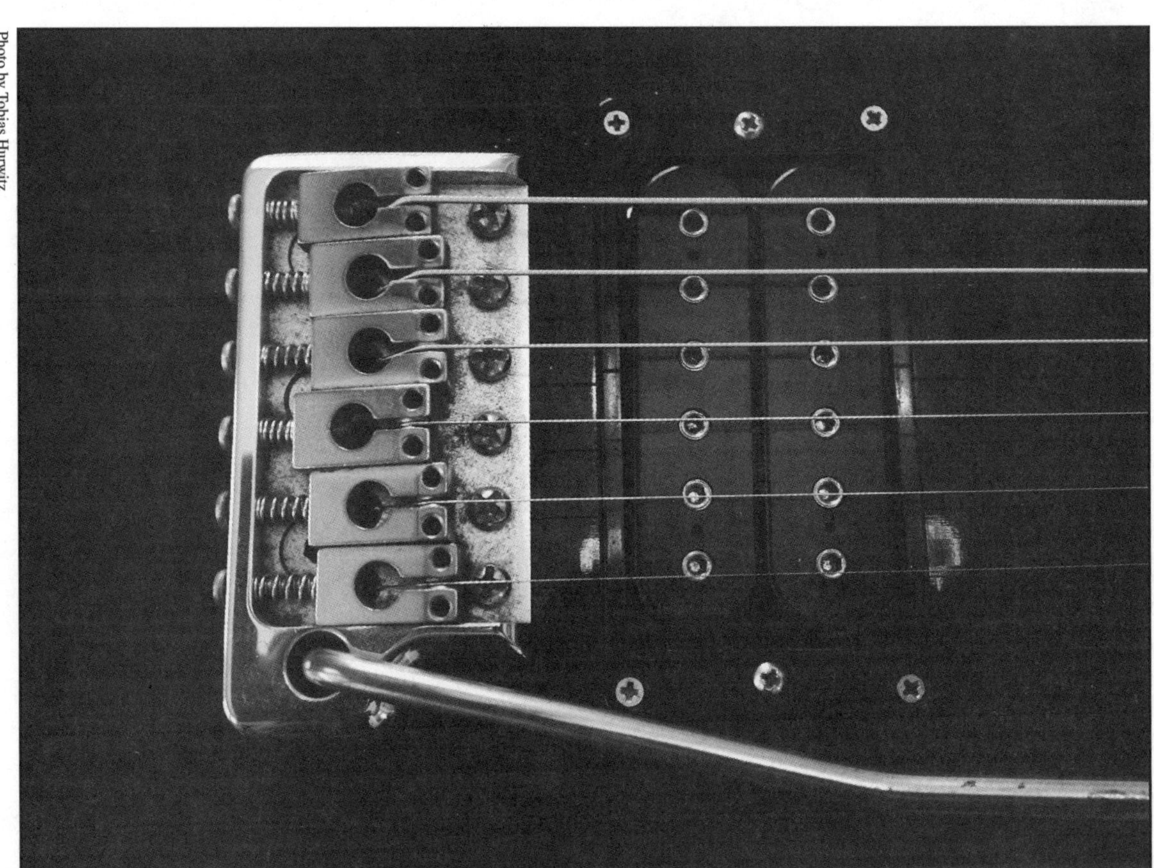

Photo by Tobias Hurwitz

PRS floating trem.

Locking Down a Trem (Blocking)

Many players have guitars with whammy bars they don't ever use. If the bar is *floating,* you'll encounter tuning problems when you break a string, and the pitches of other strings will change when you play harmonized bends—not to mention the hassle of having to constantly loosen and tighten the locking nut.

The tremolo system features a rectangular metal block that extends down into the guitar's body with springs attached to it. In a floating setup, the block can move a short distance in either direction before resting against the edge of the cavity of the guitar body. A block of wood or material such as cork or cardboard can be fitted into the spaces around the metal block to immobilize it. This keeps the bridge in one position and deactivates the whammy bar. This is called *blocking* the trem. If you don't use the bar, the best thing to do is block, or lock down, the trem. After blocking the trem, you can remove the whammy bar itself, the springs, and the locking parts of the nut, and the guitar will function more efficiently. It is very easy to unblock a trem to return the guitar to its original condition.

Unblocked floating trem.

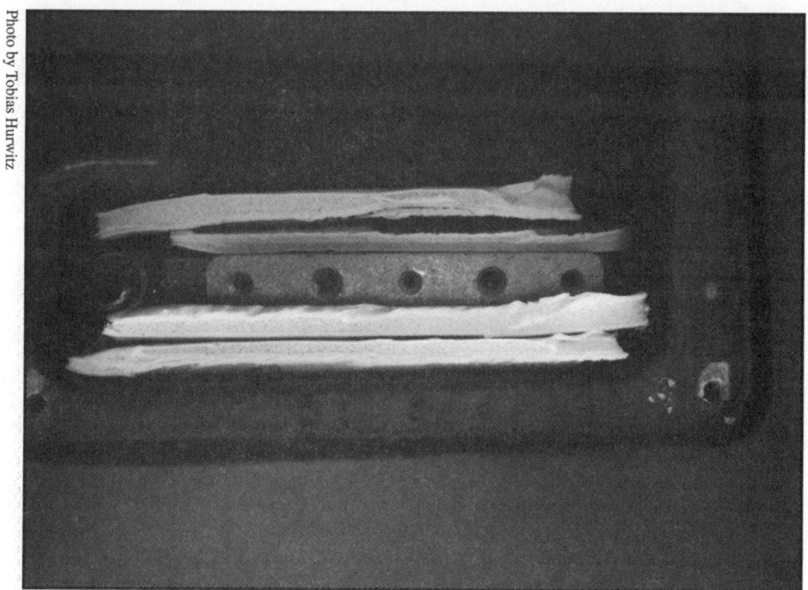

Blocked floating trem.

PART 3: THE TECHNICAL STUFF

THE SCIENCE OF SOUND

Since this book is mostly about the manipulation of sound, it's important to understand the components of sound itself. This section will cover technical terms and the concepts you will need to know.

Vibrations

- Sounds are vibrations in the air that are sensed by the ear.
- We call these vibrations *sound waves.*
- Sound waves have *pitch* (degree of highness or lowness). The pitch is determined by how quickly the vibrations happen, which is called *frequency*. This is measured in cycles per second, or *hertz* (Hz). The higher the frequency, the higher the pitch of the sound.

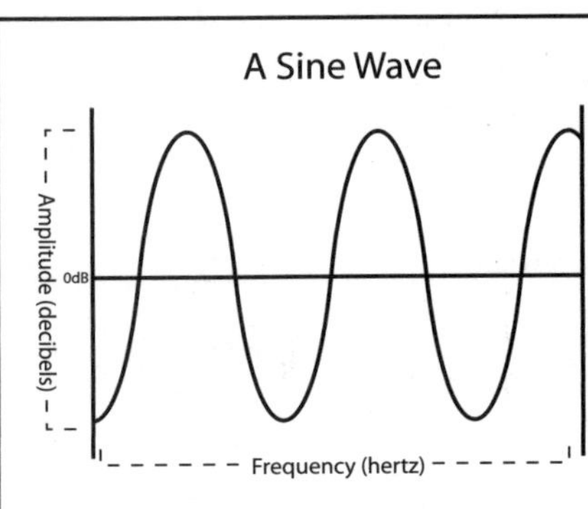

Amplitude and Types of Waves

- Another component of the sound wave is called *amplitude.* Larger more powerful waves have greater amplitude. We perceive sound waves with greater amplitude as being louder. So, amplitude = volume or level. Amplitude is usually measured in decibels (dB).
- Sound waves are often represented by *sine waves.* The sine wave in the diagram at the top right represents several cycles of a signal.
- Other wave forms are possible. For instance, a square wave—present in very distorted guitar sounds—could be represented like the diagram at the bottom right:

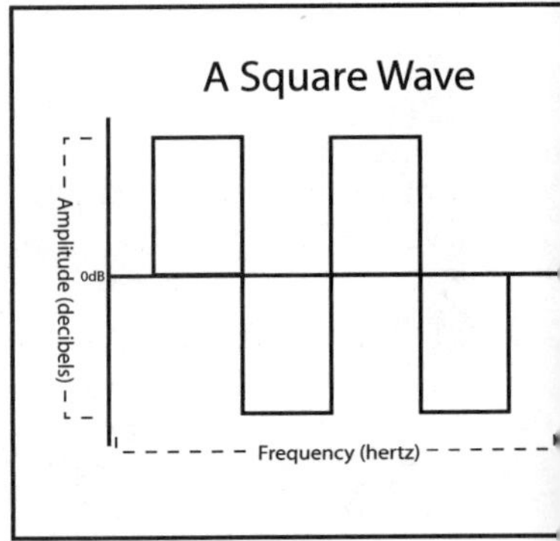

Overtones (Harmonics)

- Every note played on a musical instrument is actually made up of many parts, or *partials*— the first of which is the *fundamental tone.* The fundamental tone is the lowest partial and the perceived pitch of a note. The fundamental is accompanied by various, less-apparent tones called *harmonics,* or *overtones.*
- These additional tones fall into a structure known as the *overtone series.* The first overtone in the series is an octave above the fundamental tone, the next is a perfect 5th above that, then a perfect 4th above that, a major 3rd above that, a minor 3rd above that, and so on. (A discussion of the mathematical pattern inherent in the overtone series is beyond the scope of this book, but you can see a continuation of the series in the illustration below.)
- Variations in the amplitude and the number of overtones that augment the fundamental tone greatly affect the characteristics of the sound.

To the right is an example of the overtone series above a C fundamental tone.

The Overtone Series

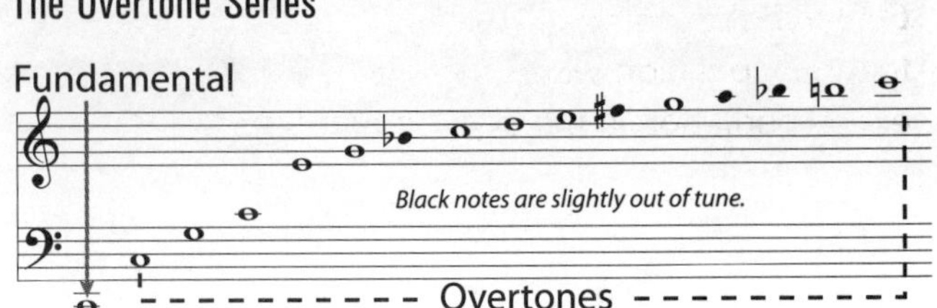

Modulation

- Components of sound waves, like frequency or amplitude, can be electronically or naturally *modulated* to produce interesting effects. Modulation is movement or change.

- Modulation of the various musical parameters can produce effects like chorusing, vibrato, flanging, and more.

- Often, an electronic signal is split. Half of it is modulated in some way (called *wet*) and is then mixed back in with the unaltered (also known as *dry*) signal. This is only one of many techniques used by audio engineers to alter sounds with effects, pedals, and processors.

Many books have been written about the physics of sound, and the more you know about sound the better.

About Block Diagrams

Block diagrams will be used throughout the rest of this book. They show how an electric guitar's signal moves through a series of devices. The direction of the signal flow is indicated by arrows. The signal usually flows from left to right. The lines connecting each piece of gear represent standard instrument cables. The settings of the knobs on the pedals and amps are also clearly indicated.

In the block diagram to the right, a Strat-style guitar is connected to a wah pedal and then to a fully cranked distortion box.

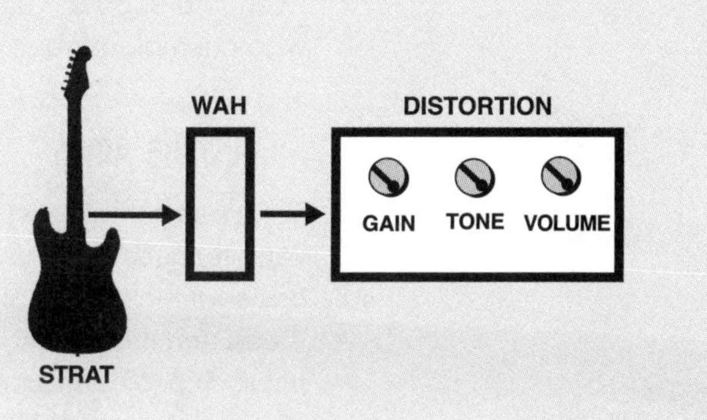

The Order of Effects

The order of pedals within a signal chain greatly affects factors such as noise level and sound quality. The signal chains in this book usually follow standard, time-tested patterns. One such chain is pictured to the right.

You will notice that reverb, delay, and chorus are placed last. This is because these effects sound better post-distortion. As long as they are placed last, the relative order of the wet effects only creates subtle changes.

The equalizer also comes post-distortion. Equalization, or simply EQ, creates less noise and functions more efficiently in this position. Distortion will pump up harmonics, filling out the guitar's frequency response. This wider response is better manipulated by the equalizer.

Observe the changes in sound that occur when you move a pedal to a new position within the chain. There are no rules. Lots of experimentation is the best path to good tone!

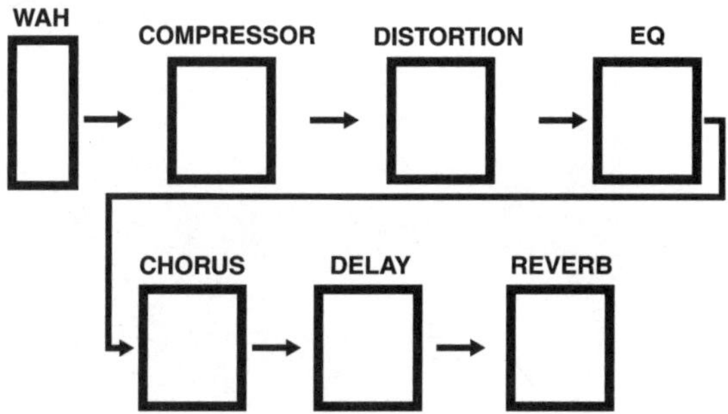

UNDERSTANDING GUITAR AMPS

An amplifier is much more than just a device which makes your guitar louder. Many consider it a musical instrument unto itself and rightly so. Guitar amps are divided into two main categories: *tube* and *solid state.* Tube amps use old-school vacuum tubes to amplify the signal, whereas solid-state amps use modern transistors. The controversy regarding the superiority of tubes over solid state, and of course digital emulation, continues to rage even after decades of research and development in these areas. Tube amps have created a huge palette of wonderfully warm and dynamic tones that are etched into our memories from decades of exposure. Tube amp sounds have been everywhere—from the jazz of Charlie Christian and the blues of B. B. King to the surf music of The Ventures and the classic rock of bands like The Beatles, The Rolling Stones, Pink Floyd, and Led Zeppelin.

Tube Amps

As a tube amp is played louder, its power tubes work harder and the result is the pleasing but elusive sound known as *power tube distortion.* Tubes are also very sensitive to playing touch (dynamic range), so it's possible to clean up a gritty sound just by playing softer. And, conversely, a player may dig in a bit harder with the pick to make the amp really growl. These two factors, power tube distortion and touch sensitivity, are the main talking points of those who champion tubes over solid state.

Solid-State Amps

Early transistorized solid-state amps didn't sound nearly as good as tube amps. They were flat, sterile, and somewhat "cold" in comparison to tube amps. Yet, the lightweight, cheap, and dependable transistor was too great a temptation for manufacturers to resist. The potential was there, and it obviously just needed some tweaking. After a lengthy period of development, the microchip joined forces with the transistor to spawn the premium solid-state and tube amps of the modern era. Newer solid-state amps incorporate digital modeling technology to closely copy the sounds of classic tube amps, speaker cabinets, stomp boxes, and more. Some of them even include an actual tube preamp, mostly as a marketing tool, but also to combine the two technologies for enhanced tone. Perhaps these new amps don't sound precisely identical to tube amps, but they are lighter, less expensive, more reliable, and sound great nonetheless.

Modern tube amps feature many improvements like multi-mode channels, MIDI switching, digital reverb, and variable wattage control. Tube amps, solid-state amps, and digital modeling amps are all available as combo amps, or as separate speakers and amp heads. We'll discuss these options next.

The Combo Amp

The *combo amp* combines the amplifier and speaker into one convenient package. Combo amps range in size from very small practice amps to large powerful ones ready for the stadium stage. They can be simple or heavily laden with features. The one pictured below is called a 2x12 because it's loaded with two 12" speakers. 1x12 and 1x10 configurations are also common.

The Vox AC30 2x12 combo pictured here was used by both John Lennon and George Harrison throughout their early work with The Beatles.

Amp Heads and Stacks

A half stack combines a separate amp head with a single 4x12 speaker cabinet. Separate amp heads often have more features than combos and can be easily matched with different speakers to achieve a variety of sounds. Amp heads are often paired with several cabinets to create full stacks, which can be seen chained together at stadium rock shows, or they may be matched with smaller cabs for studio sessions or small gigs.

Marshall JVM 100-Watt Half Stack.

Fancy Modern Amps: The Marshall JVM 100-watt half stack (see photo on page 85) features four foot-switchable channels, each of which has three modes and individual digital reverb controls. It has two master volumes, which means any of its four channels can be individually boosted by hitting a foot switch, or all four can be turned up or down simultaneously with a rotary knob. The back panel features MIDI ports for integration with other devices, two effects loops (one is foot-switchable), and a compensated direct-out jack which enables pristine recording without the use of a speaker cabinet or microphone.

Basic Amp Features

The average player may not need all the extra features found on a flagship Marshall or Mesa/Boogie amp. Amplifiers these days may have a lot of features, but when you shop for an amp there a few basic features to look for: channel switching, reverb, and an effects loop. *Channel switching* allows the user to switch (via a foot switch) between one channel that might be set for a clean rhythm sound and another channel that might be set for a louder, distorted lead sound. Channel switching makes the amp much more versatile when playing live. Basic two-channel models are the most common, but three- and four-channel amps are also available to offer even more versatility.

Reverb creates a soft, spacious sound that is essential to surf, country, jazz, rock, blues, and metal music. It's ideal for each channel of an amp to have its own reverb knob, since higher amounts of gain will dampen or suppress reverb.

The *effects loop* is a feature that players might not understand right away but will certainly appreciate when its full capacity becomes apparent. If you love the distortion tone on your amp's lead channel but also want to use delay, chorus, or another wet effect with it, then the effects loop is your solution. Effects pedals or devices can be patched into the loop, thereby inserting them post-distortion, which is the proper place for wet effects in the signal chain. Plugging directly into the effects return jack of the loop allows players who use floor-based multi-effect units to bypass the preamp section of the amp and use only the power amp section, thereby getting the best tone possible from their gear.

Boutique Amps

Boutique amplifiers became very popular in the 1990s and have since become a force to be reckoned with in the industry. These small batches of handmade tube amps are intended to be of a higher quality than what is available from major manufacturers. Boutique amps tend to feature a heavy-duty chassis, class-A operation, point-to-point wiring, high-end speakers, leather corners, custom colors, and low- or variable-wattage settings. Trainwreck, Matchless, Budda, Fuchs, and Bruno are some of the most popular boutique amp companies, and there are dozens more emerging.

Point-to-Point Wiring

In the 1950s, the recently invented printed circuit board, or PCB, began replacing the labor-intensive point-to-point wiring methods that were the norm at the time. So, roughly, the first two decades of guitar amp production exclusively featured point-to-point wiring, and virtually everything else after was made with printed circuit boards. Today, boutique amp companies like Matchless offer small batches of handmade point-to-point tube amps. Occasionally, major companies like Fender or Marshall will produce a limited-edition run of point-to-point amps that faithfully reproduce the exact specs of a favorite vintage amp.

Many of the most desirable vintage amps contained printed circuit boards and their tones were actually better in some ways because point-to-point amps needed more shielding to avoid noise problems. Amps with point-to-point wiring are also harder to service because troubleshooting them is more difficult, and the repair will usually take longer due to its complex nature. On the up side, anyone offering a point-to-point amp today is doing so with the goal of making a better amplifier. These pricey little gems are likely to deliver cool and quirky features, great looks, great tones, and very fine craftsmanship. They are shielded carefully so if there is indeed an audible difference in the thicker gauge hand-soldered wiring, you'll be able to hear it. On the flip side, there are those among us who believe point-to-point amps are simply overpriced and overrated, and that the printed circuit board took over because it's cheaper and actually works better.

How to Chain Amps Together

When guitarists like Stevie Ray Vaughan use 10 or so amps at once, they're actually *chaining* them together. To chain amps together, plug your guitar into input 1 on the front panel of an amp, then use input 2 as an output to send the signal to the next amp. The process is then repeated to form a chain of amps. The same method was used by Jimi Hendrix to create his famed walls of Marshalls. The effects send or preamp output can also be used to drive additional amps. (For more on amps and effects loops, see the chapters on Understanding Speaker Cabinets, Ohmage and Impedance, Tubes, and Signal Flow and Level.)

UNDERSTANDING SPEAKER CABINETS

Cabinets

The term *cabinet* refers to a separate enclosure that houses speakers. Guitar speaker cones are commonly available in 10", 12", and 15" sizes. Sizes smaller than 10" are usually reserved for combo amps. The term 4x12 means there are four 12" speakers in the cabinet; 2x10 indicates two 10" speakers, etc. Common speaker cabinet configurations are: 1x12, 2x12, 4x12, 4x10, and 1x15. Cabinets can be used as speakers for rack systems and as additional, auxilary amplification for combo amps. They are mostly found as components in half stacks, full stacks, or larger amp systems.

Speaker Cones

Discriminating players demand high performance from their speakers. Some speaker cones add distortion, while others produce crystal-clear jazzy tones. The lower the wattage of a speaker, the more crunch (distortion) it will yield in high-volume situations. A Marshall 4x12 cabinet loaded with 25-watt Celestion speakers will distort much more quickly than the same cabinet loaded with 75-watt Celestions. If you prefer loud clean sounds, you will be best off with speakers made by a company that specializes in that area, such as Electro Voice. Most manufacturers offer a range of speaker options.

Open Back or Closed Back?

Fans of big, crunchy sounds usually prefer closed-back cabinets. The closed-back design causes sound waves to project with force from the front of the speaker. This helps create that chest-thumping quality of great rock and roll tone. Open-back cabinets allow sound waves to radiate from both sides, resulting in a more airy or ambient sound. This is typical of jazz, blues, and pop styles. Cabinets are available with removable panels for easy conversion. Companies like Budda and Mesa/Boogie also offer split cabinets, which are half open.

Open Back

Rear view of a Peavey 1x12 extension cabinet with the panel removed for open-back operation.

Closed Back

This Marshall 4x12 cabinet features a closed back.

Split Back

Here is a rear view of a Budda 4x12 cabinet with a half-open back. There are two more speakers in the lower, closed section.

OHMAGE AND IMPEDANCE

The most important thing a guitarist should know in regards to *ohmage* is the way it affects how you connect a speaker cabinet or cabinets to an amp head. If you do it wrong, severe damage to the amp may occur. In fact, the amp may even catch on fire. Speakers are rated with ohmage values (e.g., 4 ohms, 8 ohms, 16 ohms, etc.) that reflect the electronic resistance of the speaker. Sometimes the speaker has several input jacks for selecting different ohmage loads and there may even be a toggle switch to select mono or stereo operation. To make matters more complicated, amps usually have three-way ohmage selector switches with settings for 4, 8, and 16 ohms. Some amps have multiple speaker outputs that are clearly labeled with various safe speaker combinations. Below are a couple of basic rules to follow.

Hooking Up One Speaker: This is very straightforward. Match the ohmage selector on the amp to the ohmage of the speaker, and plug it into the correct jack on the speaker. (The speaker may have more than one jack with different ohmages.)

Hooking Up Two Speakers: The ohmage selector must be set for half of the value of each speaker. For example: when hooking up two 16 ohm cabs, set the selector for 8 ohms. When connecting two 8 ohm cabinets, set the ohmage selector for 4 ohms, etc.

TUBES

Vacuum tubes, or valves, as they are called in England, have been a central component in guitar amp design since the dawn of the industry. Today, all amps either use tubes or attempt to imitate the sound tube amps have produced over the years.

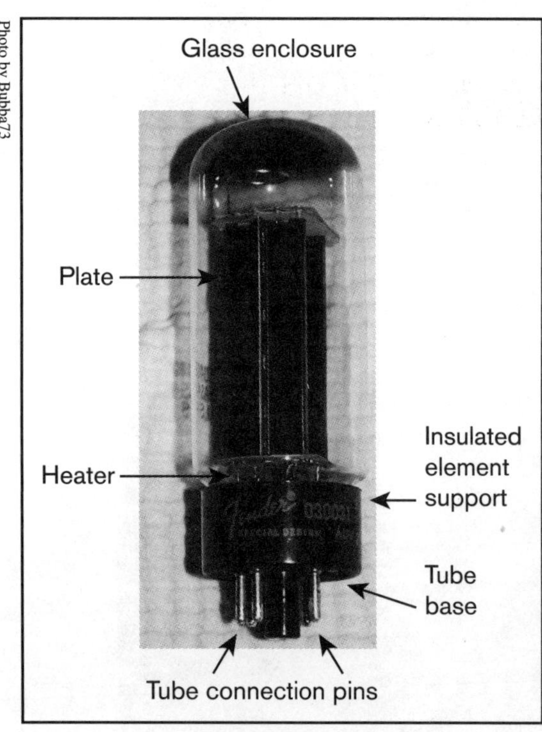

Vacuum tube with parts labeled.

Inside a Vacuum Tube

There are four main active electronic elements inside a vacuum tube: the plate, control grid, cathode, and heater (or filament, as it is sometimes called). The vacuum tube's glass enclosure creates a sealed-off environment in which these parts can heat up without burning. Preamp tubes essentially act as amplifiers that take the low voltage output of a guitar's pickup and transform it into a higher voltage signal that is strong enough to be processed by the preamp controls. The output tubes, which are also called the power tubes, then boost the signal even more, so it's strong enough to drive a speaker cabinet. The harder the tubes work, the hotter they glow and the faster they burn out.

There are three parts in an amp that commonly use tubes and they are: the preamp, power amp, and rectifier. (We'll discuss the rectifier on page 92.) Other circuits, such as the reverb unit or effects loop, may sometimes be driven or buffered by preamp tubes.

Preamp Tubes

The preamp section of a tube amp is the first thing a guitar signal passes through on its way to the speaker. Preamp tubes increase the wattage of the signal so it can then be processed by the preamp controls, which typically include gain, bass, midrange, and treble. The preamp stage is where distortion is primarily generated, and it may require several preamp tubes to achieve enough distortion—it all depends on the amp and the amount of gain desired. Preamp tubes do not need to be matched or *biased* (a concept we'll cover on page 92), so they can be replaced like light bulbs. The most common type of preamp tube for guitar amps is the 12AX7.

Power Amp Tubes

Guitar power amps commonly come in two types, *class A* and *class B*. Class-A amps operate with only one power tube and therefore have a lower wattage output than class-B amps. Class-B amps require a matched pair of at least two power tubes. The "push-pull" circuit at the heart of this design requires equal numbers of matched tubes on either side, so it will run on two, or four tubes, depending on the power output requirements. Class-A amps are free of the distortion that is an artifact of the push-pull design of class-B amps. In a nutshell, class-A amps create lower power, but more pure sound. Class-B amps are common and create the higher wattage levels that most people use. The EL34 and 6L6 are the most common types of power tubes for guitar amps.

Biasing

Unlike preamp tubes, power tubes cannot be changed easily. Power tubes must be biased by a qualified technician so that the power level of each tube is properly matched. The cost of maintenance that needs to be done regularly is one of the drawbacks of tube amps. How often you change your power tubes will depend on the hours and intensity of your use. With common use, expect to re-tube or re-bias roughly once a year, with a cost of about a few hundred dollars. There's some relief with Mesa/Boogie amps, which feature self-biasing circuits on some models that allow you to switch out matched sets of power tubes without re-biasing. For example, if you'd like to try 6L6 power tubes, which sound more like Fender than EL34s which deliver Marshall tone, you can select the tube type with a toggle switch and install them without any biasing. The other tubes in a guitar amp, the preamp and rectifier tubes (which we'll cover below), can be changed without biasing.

Note: *Tube amps are high-voltage devices that can electrocute you, so servicing should be done by qualified technicians. If you're switching a tube at home, turn the amp off and unplug it from the wall just to be safe. Oh, and make sure you're using the correct tube!*

Rectifiers and Rectifier Tubes

A guitar signal never passes through the *rectifier* circuit of an amp. The rectifier is a device that "rectifies," or corrects, electrical current for the high-voltage power supply, basically converting AC voltage into DC voltage. The only effect a tube rectifier has on your tone is a subtle sonic byproduct of a "sag" in the consistency of the power. This is a result of the inefficiency of a tube rectifier; a solid-state rectifier will produce better results. Some players like the sound of a tube rectifier, however, so Mesa/Boogie introduced a line of amps that give the user the option to switch between tube and solid-state rectifiers. We recorded the results so you can hear for yourself. You may notice the solid-state rectifier produces a tighter, louder, and brighter sound than the tube rectifier.

 **Track 16**   Solid-state rectifier

 **Track 17**   Tube rectifier

SIGNAL FLOW AND LEVEL

The terms *signal flow* and *signal level* refer to the order in which devices are situated in a signal chain (flow), and the amount of input and output signal sent to and from various devices (level). Putting your effects in the correct order and making sure each one is sending and receiving the right amount of signal is absolutely essential to properly configuring your rig and getting the best tones possible.

Flow

The order in which effects are placed in the signal chain greatly affects their sound, but there are no unbreakable rules. An important tip to remember, though, is gain-changing effects should come before wet effects in the signal chain. Gain-changing effects include: fuzz, overdrive, distortion, phase shifter, clean boost, EQ, compressor, wah, auto-wah, noise gate, and envelope filter (or follower). The exception is the volume pedal, which is usually placed last in line. Wet effects include: reverb, delay, chorus, flanger, harmonizer, and the whammy pedal.

An example of a tried-and-true signal chain is the following:

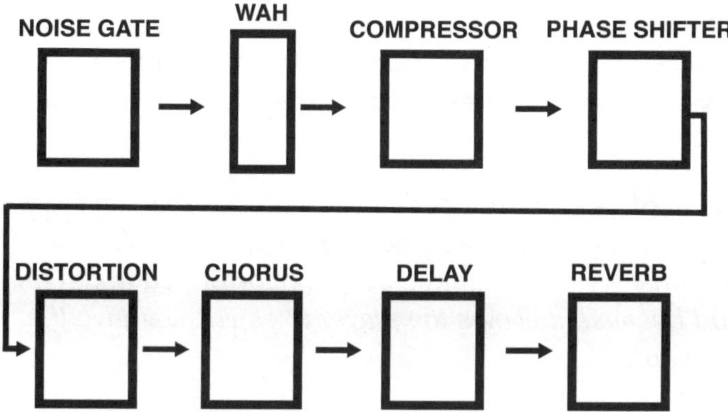

Tip: Phase shifters, flangers, and the whammy pedal may be freely moved around the signal chain without worry. They sound good anywhere, but their location before or after distortion will sound quite different. Their placement is up to the user.

Try effects in different configurations to see what you like. Sometimes a "mistake" can produce a happy accident. Try hooking up a wah pedal backwards, and you'll get the cool sound that David Gilmour stumbled upon for the song "Echoes" from *Meddle.* Gilmour discovered an effect that sounds like seagulls!

Track 18

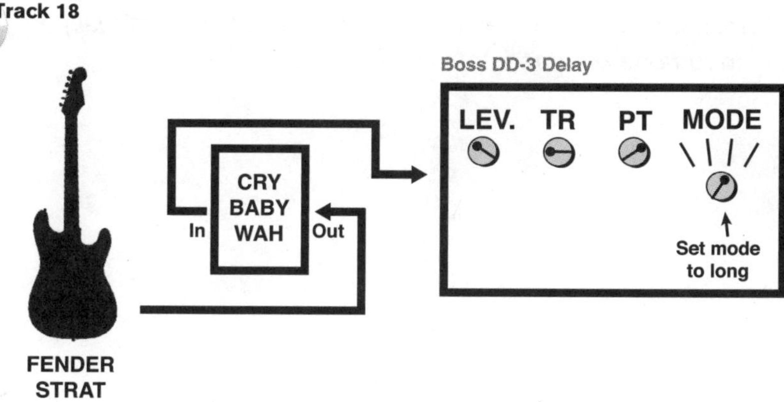

Guitar Gear Levels

There are several kinds of signal level for guitar gear.

1. **Consumer line level:** The *nominal* level, or level in which a device is designed to operate, for consumer audio is -10dBV, which means minus 10 decibels. In other words, it's very soft and perhaps a bit noisy. Consumer line level is used to transmit audio signals from CD players to amps and from one stomp box to the next.

2. **Professional line level:** The nominal level for professional audio is +4dBu, which basically means a lot louder with less background noise. Professional line level is used in rack-mounted units and other high-end gear.

High-end guitar equipment will usually include a button labeled -10/+4 near the input jack or effects loop. This must be set properly to accommodate the incoming signal, matching the gear being plugged in. If it isn't set correctly, the sound will be either very weak and distant or way too loud and unpleasantly distorted. Professional-grade gear will sometimes include input level meters or LED overload lights. Green is used to indicate healthy signal flow, and red means too much signal. Depending on the *headroom* (see definition below) of a given device, optimal levels will usually flash red once every second or so without staying all the way in the red, which is called *pegging*. A good signal is robust enough to drive the device without being so high that it distorts its input stage. Your ear will become accustomed to identifying level mismatches over time. When it sounds right, then the levels must have been set right. If expensive gear sounds horrible, check the levels!

About headroom: *Headroom is the amount of gain above nominal level (0 VU) that a device can receive before clipping. Lots of headroom is good for rack mounted delay units and similar devices whose aim is to affect a guitar's signal without adding distortion. Lower headroom on, say, the input of a guitar amp is also good because it allows the player to easily overdrive the amp with a boost pedal or high-output pickup.*

More About Effects Loops

We have previously mentioned that wet effects should come post-distortion in the signal chain. This might pose a problem if, for example, you like the distortion that comes from your amp's heavy channel but would like also to be able to use your favorite delay pedal for some sweet echo. Enter the effects loop. The effects loop inserts a signal after the preamp, which produces the distortion, but before the power amp, which amplifies the overall sound. Therefore, all wet effects should be run in the loop if amp distortion is to be used. They can also be added post-amplifier through a mixing desk during a live performance or recording session. The send of the loop goes to the input of the wet effect, and the return of the loop is connected to the output of the wet effect.

Trick of the trade: *If you wish to bypass the preamp section of a guitar amp and only use it as a power amp, then plug your guitar directly into the effects return jack. Players who use multi-effect units should not plug them straight into the front of an amp. Multi-effects units usually include preamps, and it's not ideal to run one preamp into another.*

NOISE

If there's one thing electric guitarists actually agree on, it's that noise is bad and the less of it in your guitar sound the better.

Let's first learn about the terms used to describe noise. There is always a small amount of noise inherent in most audio signals. This is called the *noise floor*. Think of when you plug a guitar with a single-coil pickup into a loud amp and don't play anything but still hear some noise. That is the noise floor. Now if you strum a chord, chances are you won't notice the noise while the chord is ringing, because the chord is so much louder than the noise. The chord is called the *signal.* The difference between the volume of the chord and the volume of the noise is called *signal-to-noise ratio.* As the chord fades, the noise becomes more apparent and there will be a point where the chord becomes lower in volume than the noise. This is the *threshold.* Most of us simply turn the volume knob down on our guitar when a note or chord fades away. This silences the noise at the threshold point. There is a device that does this automatically, and it is called a *noise gate.* A noise gate is the most popular way to deal with noise. A noise gate is the most popular way to deal with noise, and it usually functions best when placed first in the signal chain. That way, it works just like turning the volume knob down on your guitar.

- *Sensitivity* sets the threshold at which the gate closes.

- *Decay* controls the speed of the gate closing.

Noise Reduction

Gadgets like the Rocktron Pro Hush II are called *noise reduction* units. They combine frequency-specific gating technology with downward expansion technology and work even better than simple noise gates. Noise reduction units actually improve the signal-to-noise ratio instead of merely silencing the noise before the signal starts and after it fades (as a noise gate would do). Units like the Pro Hush II function best in the effects loop of an amp or somewhere in the effects chain after which the noise has been introduced in the signal. If you're running an old-school rack system with many units chained together and simultaneously responding to the commands of a MIDI foot controller, this is the way to go. Noise reduction units work quite splendidly and can be bypassed or set to handle anything from slight noise to heavy noise.

Noise Is Everywhere

Noise can come from many sources. It could come from gain-altering devices, like compressors or distortion pedals, or from a bad tube in your amp. Noisy single-coil pickups, inadequate shielding inside the body cavity of your guitar, or too many tangled wires and wall-wart power adapters contribute to noise problems. Noise can come from your rig being close to appliances like light fixtures. The electricity which powers your rig can be "dirty" due to the ground wire picking up noise. Noise is everywhere and results from a combination of many different factors.

Listen to the audio tracks to determine what you should use to clean up noise.

Track 19   This lick is noisy!

Track 20   Here's the same track with a Boss NF-1 gate.

Track 21   And now again, with Waves X-Noise and X-Humm plug-ins.

Scrubbing the Noise

Noise can also be removed from a recorded track by *scrubbing* the track. The sections of noise floor that are recorded before the guitar starts playing and all the little gaps of noise between notes can be deleted by an audio engineer through editing. The engineer would cross-fade the beginning and end of some or all of the notes to make the editing sound natural. When reverb is applied to the track after scrubbing, it fills each gap with depth, helping to glue it all together into a perfectly natural sound.

Track 22   This is the same track as above with only scrubbing, showing you that we can always just "fix it in the mix."

Boss Noise Gate NF-1 pedal.

Ebtech Hum Eliminator.

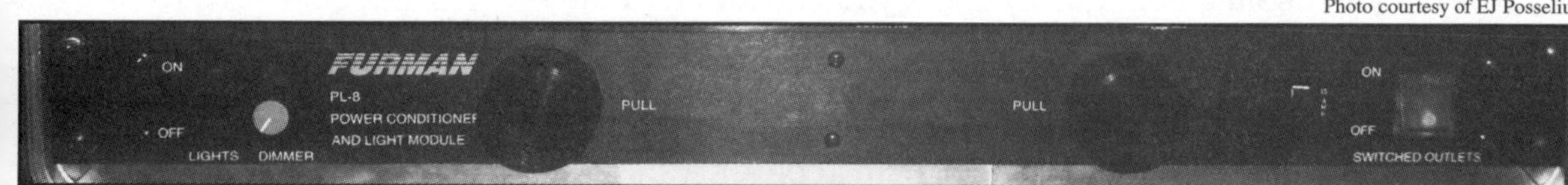

Furman Power Conditioner.

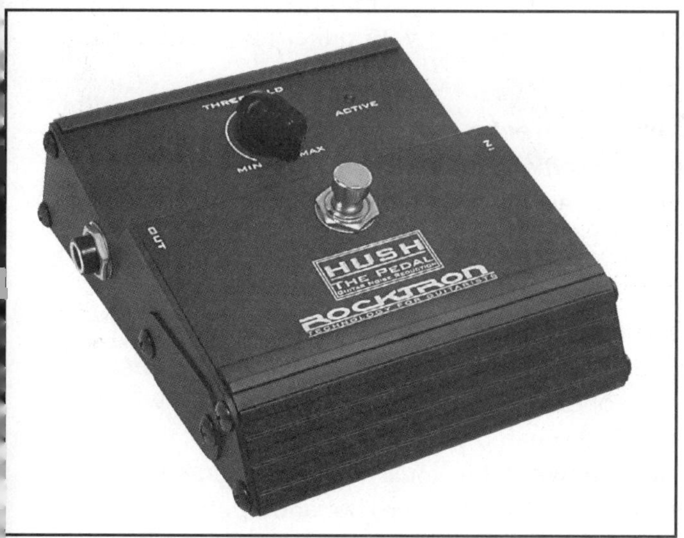

Rocktron's HUSH Pedal.

Other Ways to Reduce Noise in Your Rig

If possible, it's best to build a rig that avoids the need for noise gates or noise reduction. These units are costly, take up valuable space on a pedalboard or in a rack system, and must be set correctly to avoid unpleasant side effects. In the case of the noise gate, the tail end of sustained notes may flutter or be abruptly cut off. Noise reduction can dull the overall tone and also shorten sustain if used too much. I must admit that sometimes I'm driven to use these devices, but not if I can avoid it. Let's break down other ways to reduce noise in your rig.

Power: All grounded appliances in most buildings are essentially connected through the ground wire, which is the third wire—the one with the longest prong in a three-prong plug. Any noise-causing interference generated by such appliances is called "dirt". Use a quality power conditioner to eliminate dirt in the power. High-end power conditioners have digital voltage readouts, so you can tell if the power is weak or in flux. If the power is too high, the conditioner will limit voltage to 110. If it's too low, the power will be boosted by battery backup to the desired 110 volts. Power conditioners will help your rig run noise-free. Also, check for a ground lift switch on your amp, processor, or power supply. It can eliminate the *60 cycle hum* caused by ground loops. The 60-cycle hum and other noise problems may also be eliminated by power conditioning.

Note: The United States uses a 110 volt/60 hertz standard power system, while Europe uses a 220volt/50 hertz system. Some American made guitar gear comes equipped to work with the European system, but most does not.

Cabling: Shorter cables and cables with heavier gauges will produce less noise, so always try to use the best quality cable you can afford at the shortest possible length cable you'll need.

Single-coil pickups: If you're playing a vintage Strat-style guitar with a five-position blade switch, there will be single-coil hum in pickup positions 1, 3, and 5. Remember, positions 2 and 4 combine adjacent pickups for a "humbucking" sound that kills the noise. Noiseless single-coil pickups now come standard on many Stratocasters and are available as replacement pickups. They are dead quiet and sound great!

Shielding: The electronics cavity in your electric guitar is supposed to be covered with shielding that has been painted on, foil taped, or both. If it isn't properly done, there will be noise problems. Have a skilled technician look over your guitar to make sure it's properly shielded.

Too much gain from combining the wrong effects: Running two distortion pedals together or combining a compressor and a distortion pedal will likely cause a lot of noise. Running a hot signal from an active pickup can also throw off the gain balance in your rig and make everything sound noisy. You may have to work with less distortion and sustain to enjoy a low-noise system.

Tubes: Tubes wear out eventually and sometimes become *microphonic*. A tube that is microphonic can produce noise or feedback. Tapping on your tubes gently, while the amp is on, will reveal a bad tube if you have one. When you tap on a bad tube, it will make a ringing sound. If the offending tube is a preamp tube, you can replace it without re-biasing or retubing the whole amp. If it's a power tube, you'll need to replace all of the power tubes and possibly re-bias the amp. Obviously, tubes are hot and operate at high voltage. So be very careful, or just have an authorized technician deal with your tubes.

Take notice of these preventative measures, and you may never need a noise gate or reducer.

PHYSICAL AND VIRTUAL EFFECTS

Knowing about physical effects will be tremendously useful when you have to program their counterparts in the virtual world. As we already know, physical effects exist in every form—from stomp boxes and tape echoes to rack-mounted units and everything in between. Play with the knobs on stomp boxes and get to know the wiring of amps, mics, and pedalboards. The experience gained will help you better understand virtual effects when you encounter them in plug-ins and software.

Since the names of the actual effects units are trademarked, companies like Line 6 and Roland use clever monikers to refer to the gear they are emulating. For instance, a "Script Phaser" is a clone of a vintage MXR Phase 90 that features the script logo. A "Modern California" amp refers to a Mesa/Boogie Mark IV, or similar, amp.

Below, we have illustrated a simple signal chain on a pedalboard.

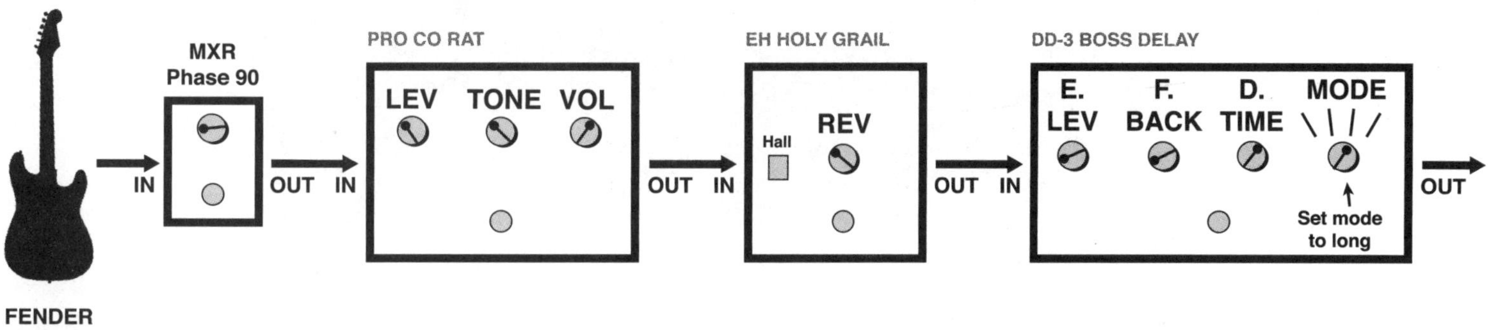

Here is the same signal chain as above but displayed on the "grid" page of the Axe-Edit software provided by Fractal Audio Systems for their Axe-FX II processor. When you click on an individual pedal in the software, its controls are accessed via a drop-down screen. Note how the virtual compressor has the same three knobs as the real one.

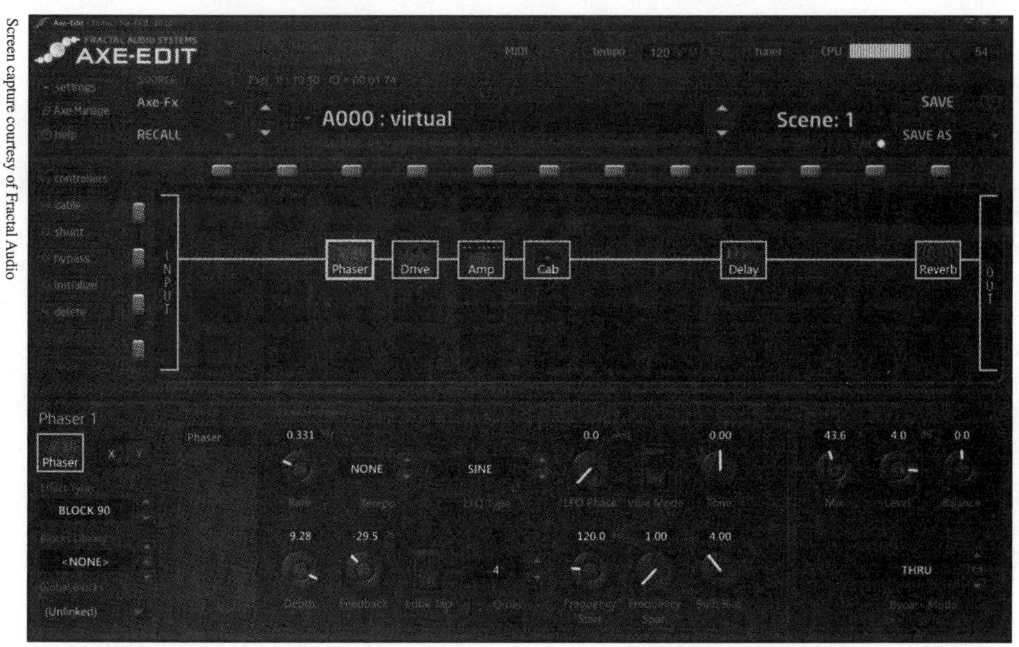

Axe-FX II screen.

The AmpliTube app for the iPhone or iPad can create the same signal chain that we've been studying. See below.

AmpliTube app tor the iPod or iPad.

This signal chain, or any other, can be easily created in various digital environments. But do the digital models stack up to the real thing? You decide. Here's a lick played through the three different systems we have discussed in this chapter. Hearing how they sound should shed some light on the subject.

 **Track 23** Real Pedals

 **Track 24** Fractal Simulation

 **Track 25** Amplitube Simulation

It will be up to you to decide which sounds more authentic. After you listen for authenticity, you should probably decide which actually sounds better. At some point, technology must evolve beyond tubes and tangled wires. Do you really want to hear the hum of questionable power supplies and aging wires, lug all of that stuff around and fix it as it constantly breaks? Companies specializing in digital products, like Apple, Roland, Line 6, and Fractal Audio, would like to have you believe that the time has finally come to retire your tube amps, cabs, mics, and pedals. This continues to be a controversial issue. Only time will tell if the tube amp will go the way of the VCR or 8-track player.

CABLING

There are three types of cables that will fit into the output jack of your electric guitar, but only the ¼" shielded *instrument cable* is the correct choice. Shielded ¼" instrument cables are used to plug guitars into amps and pedals into each other. They have one ring on the male tip and usually say "instrument cable" on the side.

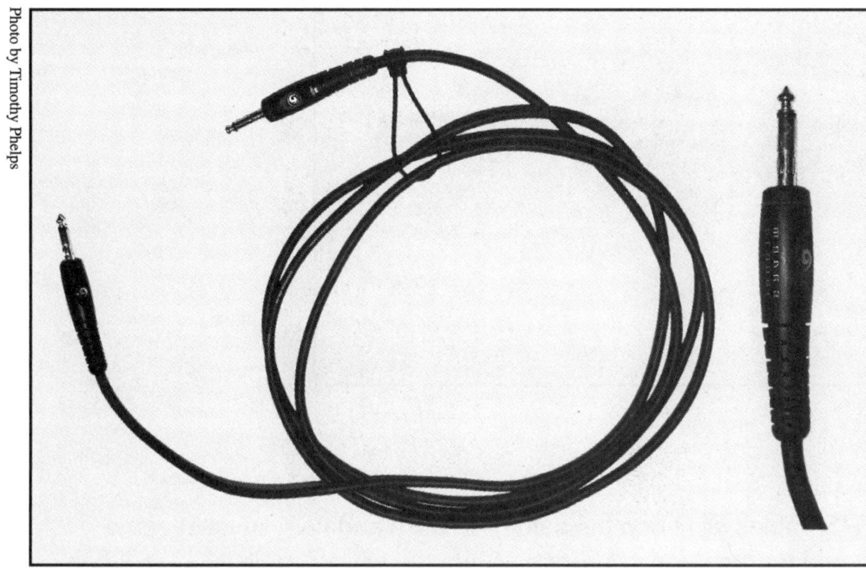

¼" instrument cable.

Don't confuse a *speaker cable* with the instrument cable. Speaker cables have one ring on the male tip, and they usually say "speaker cable" on the side. Some speaker cables feature two cables molded together like a small extension cord. Speaker cables should only be used to connect the output of an amplifier to the input of a speaker.

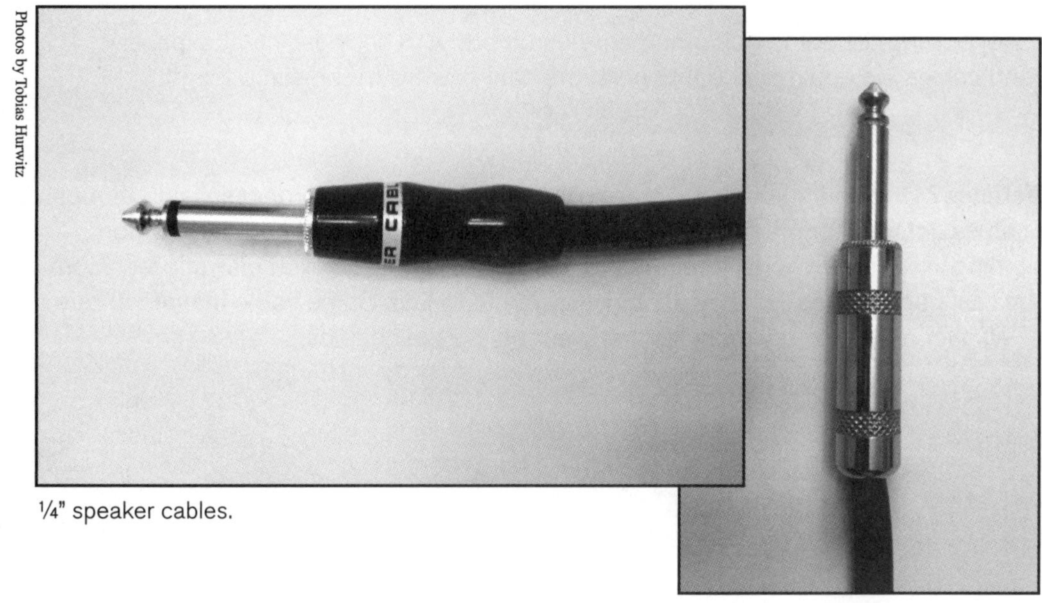

¼" speaker cables.

The third type of cable is the *TRS cable*, sometimes called a balanced stereo cable. (The "T" stands for tip, "R" stands for ring, and "S" represents sleeve.) TRS cables have two rings on the male ¼" tip, and they are used to connect expression pedals, foot switches, and rack-mounted gear.

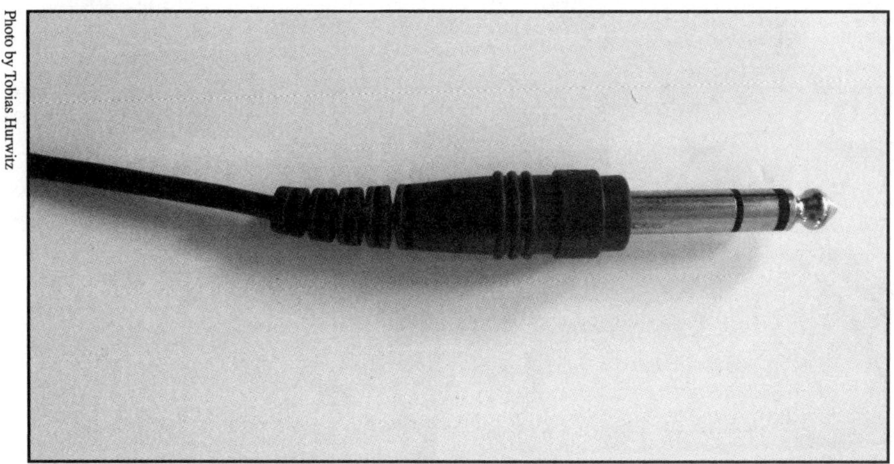

TRS cable.

Instrument, speaker, and TRS cables all fit into the same ¼" jacks and carry at least some signal—even when being used for the wrong purpose. When the wrong cable is used, it can result in damage to amplifiers, and a weak, noisy tone.

Cable Test

Many companies would like you to believe thicker, more expensive cables with gold ends produce superior sound, so here's a little detective work.

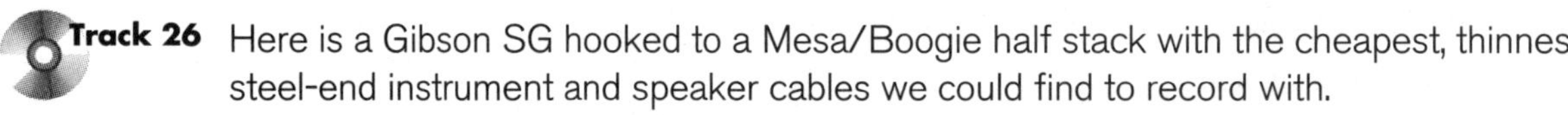 **Track 26** Here is a Gibson SG hooked to a Mesa/Boogie half stack with the cheapest, thinnest steel-end instrument and speaker cables we could find to record with.

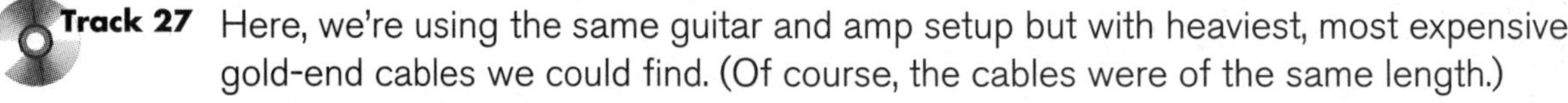 **Track 27** Here, we're using the same guitar and amp setup but with heaviest, most expensive gold-end cables we could find. (Of course, the cables were of the same length.)

Is there a difference? Decide for yourself. Amazingly, everyone at the recording session thought the cheaper cables actually sounded better. Simply put, they had a clearer and brighter tone, and lacked nothing in terms of overall frequency response. Nonetheless, you may still feel more secure with heavier cables because they're obviously made to last. Some cable manufacturers, like Monster, will offer a free-replacement lifetime warranty on their cables.

PART 4: REAL RIGS AND WHAT THEY CAN DO

REAL RIGS

People who write books about guitar gear tend to own lots of gear or operate tons of it on a day-to-day basis. With so much gear to choose from, gear enthusiasts will often put together different rigs for various situations. The following is a breakdown of three types of rigs.

Small Rig

First, let's take a look at a small rig, which can operate on AC or battery power. This rig can travel to the beach, easily squeezing between boogie boards and duffle bags in the back of a car, and is inexpensive enough that you may not care if it gets wet. The whole rig can be carried in one light trip, so you can play campfires, parties, song circles, and small rehearsals with it. You could also throw this rig in the car as a spare in case your real rig breaks down at an inopportune moment.

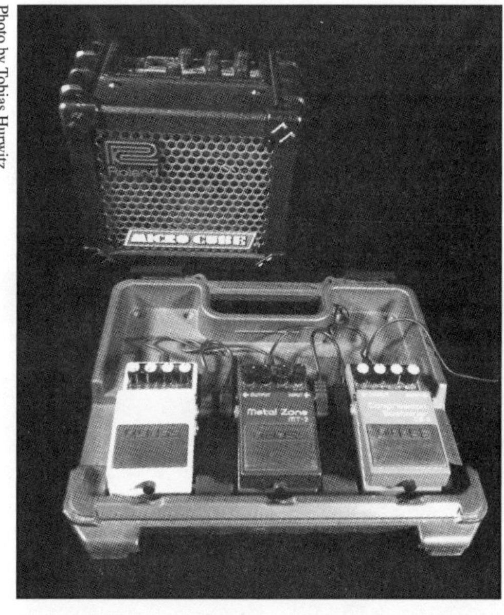

Photo by Tobias Hurwitz

A small rig.

Small Rig Breakdown

    Amp: Roland Microcube

    Pedalboard: Boss BCB-30

    Pedals: Boss CS-3 Compressor, Boss MT-2 Metal Zone, DD-3 Digital Delay

The Roland Microcube is equipped with COSM amp-modeling technology and onboard effects. Check out these tracks for some small-rig tone samples.

Track 28   Clean Rhythm Guitar

Track 29   Clean Compressed Lead

Track 30   Metal Lead

Track 31   Cascade Delay

Medium Rig

Now let's check out an example of a medium rig. This rig features a Mesa/Boogie 5:25 Express 1x10" amp finished in red lizard skin and brown leather with an SKB-124 pedalboard that includes a killer arsenal of pedals. Even though the amp has two channels, various foot-switchable functions, and many fancy features, the best approach might be to simply set to it a clean warm sound with a little reverb. All the tone variation will come from the pedalboard.

For blues or jazz jams, simply take the amp without the pedalboard, but bring along the amp's foot switch so you can go between channels. It's great to be able to bring an amp that you can carry with one hand and still be loud enough to play with a drummer! A delay pedal like the Boss DD-1 can also be used to add a little atmosphere.

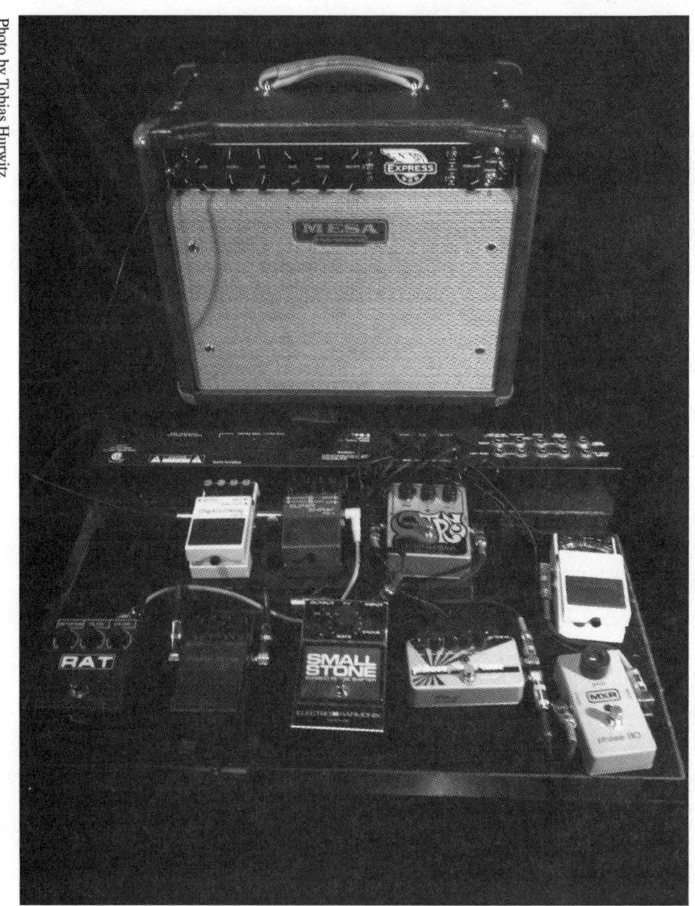

A medium rig.

Here are a few tone samples from the medium rig.

Track 32 Clean rhythm

Track 33 Slight grit

Track 34 Funky lead

Track 35 Shred lead

Track 36 Clean lead

Track 37 Metal rhythm

The "Real" Rig

Finally, let's take a look at a "real" rig. Using a device like the Fractal Audio Systems Axe-FX II along with the MFC-101 foot controller brings you into the modern world. This is the most current state-of-the-art in guitar signal processing. The system is quite different from traditional amps and pedals, as it's basically a computer housed in a two-space rackmount. The user can create virtually any combination of amps, pedals, speakers, etc., and save it into a patch.

Photos by Tobias Hurwitz

A "real" rig.

Check out these tone samples recorded, using the Axe-FX II, directly onto a hard drive without microphones, speakers, or amps.

Track 38   Slight grit

Track 39   JCM 800

Track 40   Shred lead

Track 41   Ambient

Track 42   Talk Box

Track 43   Auto wah

Track 44   Tape distortion

SETUPS FOR DIFFERENT MUSICAL STYLES

Let's look at how to achieve certain tones traditionally associated with specific genres. We'll cover blues, country, jazz, '70s classic rock, funk, heavy metal, '80s hair metal, djent, and more.

The Blues Sound

The all-American sound of the electric blues took form in the late 1940s with Muddy Waters making a name for himself and the Chicago blues. The idea was straightforward really: just take a good guitar, plug it into a good amp, and let it rip.

By the early '50s, Muddy was known to plug a P-90 equipped Les Paul Gold Top into a small Gibson tube amp and play without a pick.

To achieve an awesome, straight-amping blues tone, we plugged a 1968 Tele into a 1964 Gibson GA-20 combo. This no-nonsense tone is full of grit, grind, and gusto!

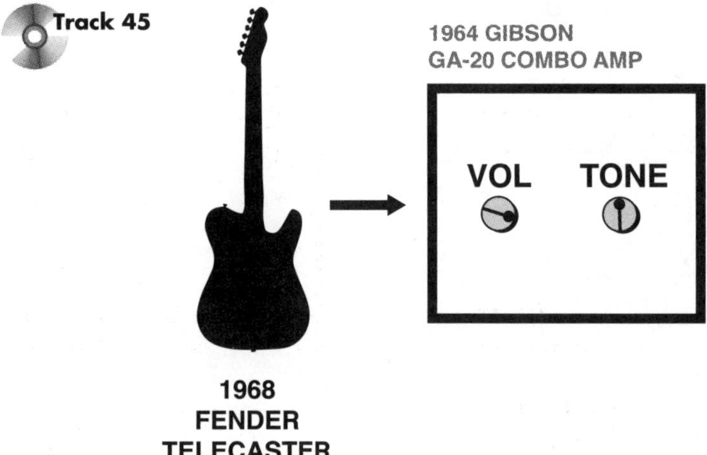

The Country Sound

The sweet sound known as "country twang"—as championed by the likes of Bill Kirchen, Danny Gatton, Scotty Moore, Vince Gill, Merle Haggard, and Waylon Jennings—is largely a Fender phenomenon. The standard procedure for getting this sound is to plug a Fender Telecaster into a Fender Twin Reverb or similar amp, and, if you want to get fancy, use a little compression and delay. A few hours in the woodshed wouldn't hurt either, since you might have to pull off a little chicken pickin' mixed in with your pedal steel–style bends!

The sound on Track 46 was achieved with a '68 Fender Tele strung with 12-gauge Ernie Balls played through a 1965 Fender Twin Reverb. In front of the amp, we used a Boss CS-3 Compressor and a Boss DD-3 Delay set at around 90 milliseconds. Have a look at the block diagram below to see the exact settings. Check it out!

Track 46

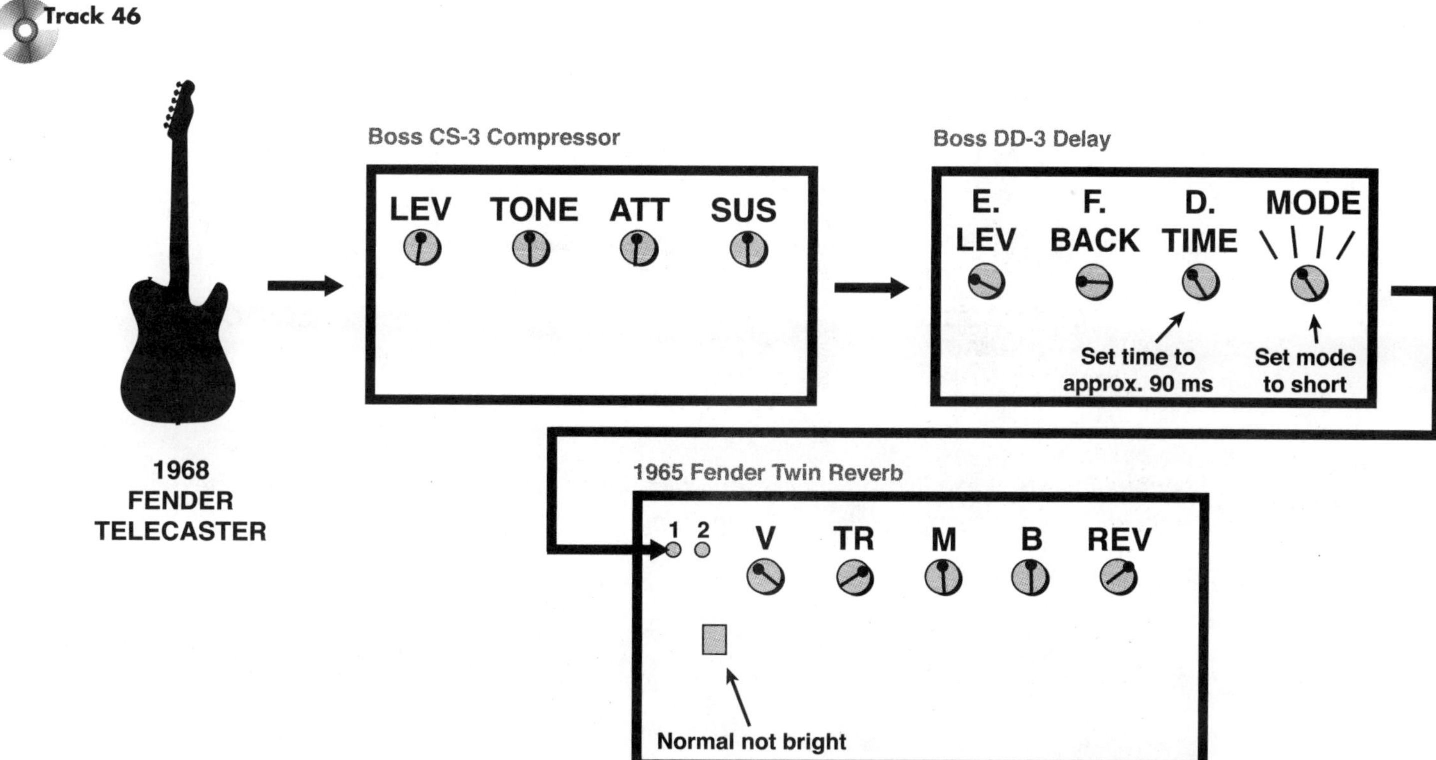

The Jazz Sound

The sound of jazz guitar is fat, warm, soft, and clean. If you can picture the tones of Joe Pass, Wes Montgomery, Charlie Christian, George Benson, or Lenny Breau, you'll realize they all have that signature jazz sound. The usual method for attaining that tone is to plug a good quality archtop into a small combo amp, roll off the top end, boost the bass, and use a little delay and/or reverb if the mood strikes you. Many jazzers, like Les Paul for example, achieve authentic jazz tones with solid-body instruments.

For this track, we plugged a Gibson SG Standard straight into a 1967 Ampeg SB-12 Portaflex combo and added a touch of reverb and delay to the mix. The guitar was strung with flatwound 11-gauge strings, and the neck pickup was used. This is one example of a totally legit jazz tone!

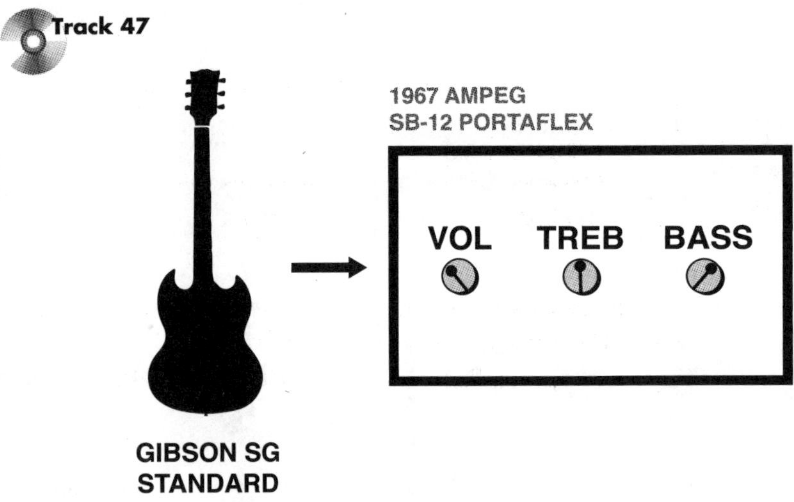

Acoustic note: Latin jazz artists like Antônio Carlos Jobim and Charlie Byrd achieved similarly soft and warm sounds by playing nylon-string acoustic guitars.

The 1970s Classic Rock Sound

1970s classic rock is a huge genre that encompasses many tones and styles. The style we're focusing on here is reminiscent of groups like Heart, Styx, Alice Cooper, Cheap Trick, Rick Derringer, Eagles, and Bad Company. Here's how to attain the classic "hard rock" sound: Plug a Les Paul into a Marshall. This type of tone has a lot of punch and a medium amount of distortion. Chords ring with clarity and a sustained note easily morphs into sweet feedback.

For Track 48, we plugged a '61 Les Paul into a '70s MXR Distortion Plus into a 1974 Marshall JMP Super Lead half stack loaded with Celestion Greenbacks, which are the most desirable vintage low-wattage 12" speakers ever to grace a Marshall cabinet. The result was magnificent!

Track 48

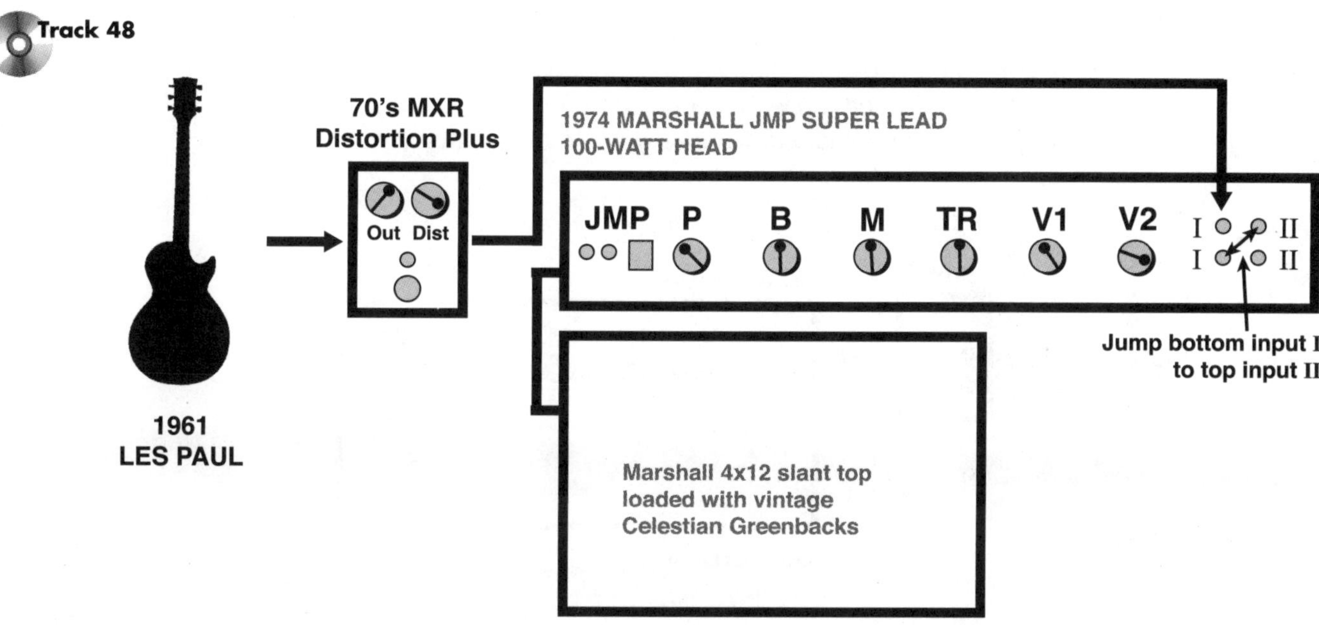

About the amp used for the recording: *The 100-watt heads in the Marshall Super Lead are coveted vintage collector's items and are sometimes referred to as "plexis," because the earlier models had a plexiglass covering over the gold faceplate. These amps produce a beautiful rock distortion tone with stunning harmonics and unusual chord clarity, which is why they've been used on so many vintage and modern recordings, including the bulk of Eddie Van Halen's early works.*

The front panel layout (pictured above) may seem confusing at first glance. The V1 (Volume 1) and V2 (Volume 2) controls work in conjunction with the four jumpable inputs on the right of the faceplate. If the inputs are not jumped, only the treble channel (TR) will be audible, and the amp will sound thin and weak. It is standard procedure to connect the bottom left input to the top right one, activating the bass channel. Then the low-end growl of the amp can be dialed in to perfection with the V2 knob. This might seem like a strange procedure, but it's just the way it was done at the time!

The Funk Sound

There's a quirky intensity among funk artists that is sometimes mirrored in their guitar tones. If you recall members of Funkadelic dressing only in giant-sized diapers or the The Red Hot Chili Peppers running onto stage with tube socks as their only garb, you'll get the idea. The funk pantheon also includes colorful characters like George Duke, Bootsy Collins, Earth, Wind & Fire, Sly Stone, Stevie Wonder, Isaac Hayes, Wild Cherry, Stanley Clarke, Prince, Chaka Kahn, and countless others.

Signature funk tones usually come into play with clean rhythm guitar since the leads are almost always '70s style hard rock. These rhythm patterns are often based on syncopated sixteenth-note strumming and the layering of *ostinato* grooves. (The term "ostinato" refers to accompaniment patterns that are repeated.) The tones include standard clean Strat sounds with wah, phaser, and compressor.

Think of Isaac Hayes' theme song to the movie *Shaft*. The clean wah riff on the rack is typical of the classic funk style. Try playing octaves in a syncopated sixteenth-note groove while tapping your foot in quarter notes on the wah—you're a funk master! Check out the setup below and listen to Track 49 for our demonstration.

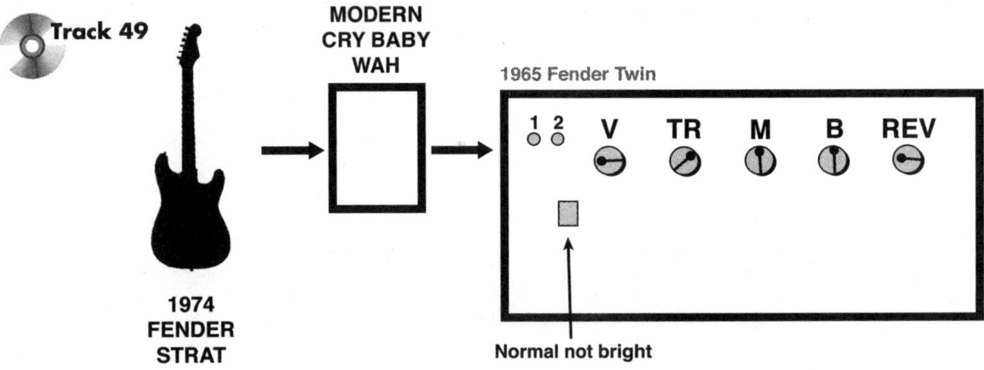

Here's another great funk tone.

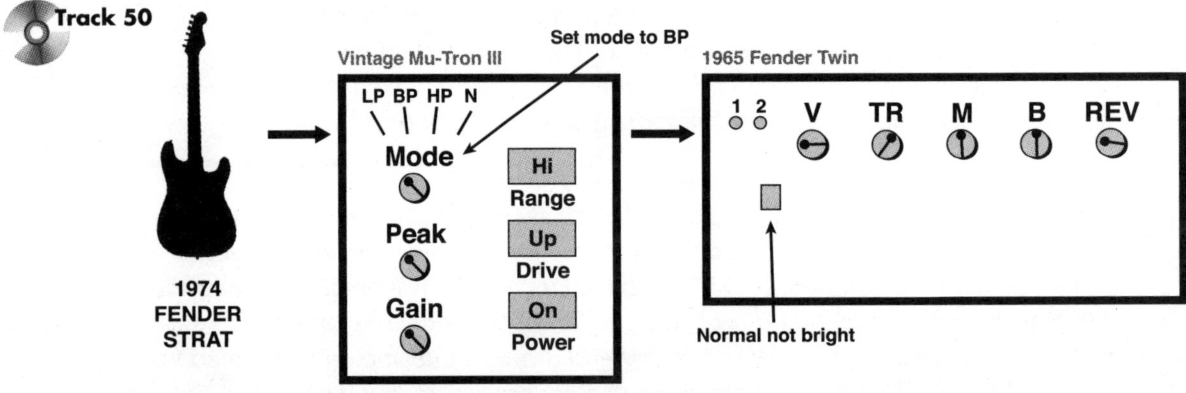

These settings yield an envelope sensitive (see note below) clean attack that screams funk with every note. If you don't have a mini Q-Tron, you can substitute a Boss Auto-Wah, Mu-Tron III, or a Pigtronix Envelope Phaser. Funk out!

Note: *Envelope sensitive effects react differently to the dynamics of a player's picking. In the case of the Mu-Tron III, the harder the picking, the more pronounced the wah effect.*

The Heavy Metal Sound

Heavy metal guitar tones are highly distorted and often so laden with other effects that they take the guitar quite far afield from its natural sound. Metal falls into at least five broad categories, each of which also have subgenres: early metal, hair metal, nu metal, metalcore, and djent.

Black Sabbath, Deep Purple, and Led Zeppelin, who laid the groundwork for today's metal, are considered early metal. Hair metal is essentially '80s music that includes Judas Priest, Van Halen, Dio, Def Leppard, Rat, and many others. Metal of the 1990s includes nu metal, tuned-down 7- and 8-string metal, death metal, some speed metal, and black metal. Slipknot, Marilyn Manson, Necrophagist, and Behemoth are all in this group. And then there's metalcore, which combines elements of different styles and eras of metal. DragonForce and Avenged Sevenfold are metalcore bands. Djent is the most modern form of metal to date and includes its founding band, Meshuggah, and newer bands such as Periphery, and Animals as Leaders.

The 1980s Hair Metal Sound

To get a good '80s hair metal tone, we plugged a double-locking trem-equipped Ibanez Xiphos guitar into an MXR Phase 90 into a Boss NF-1 Noise Gate and then into the heaviest channel of a Marshall JVM 100. We then went straight into the recorder via the compensated direct out. Of course, we scooped the mids, boosted the lows and highs, and added a small amount of echo with a Boss DD-3 Digital Delay via the amp's effects loop.

Track 51

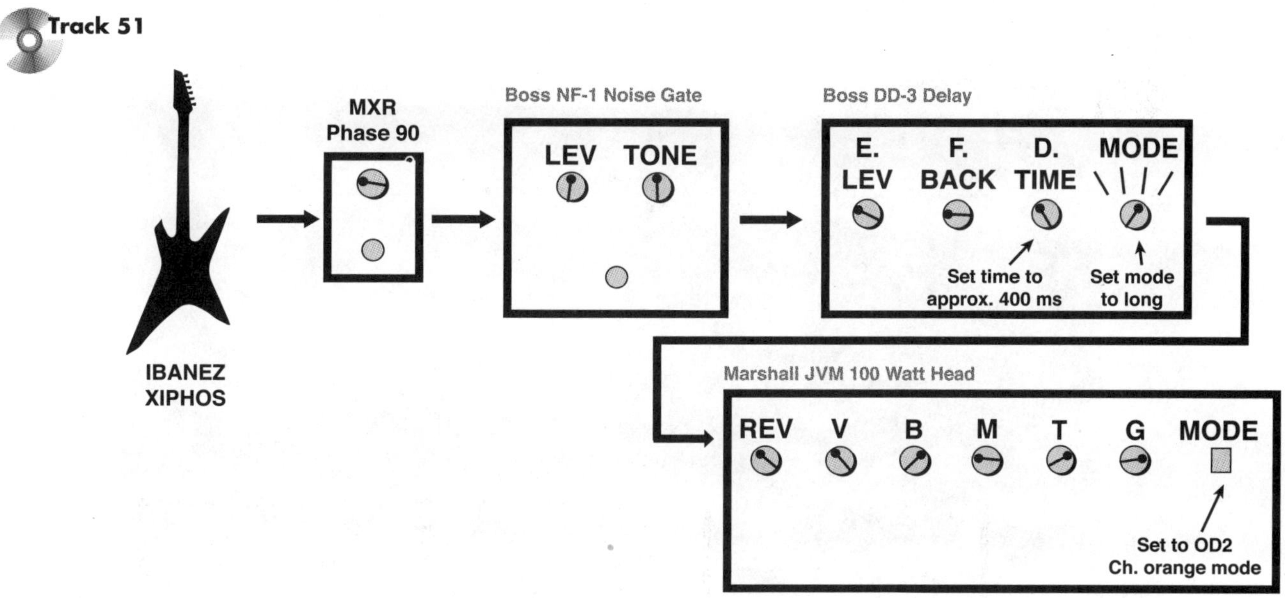

The Djent Sound

Djent (the "D" is silent) is an onomatopoeia for the sound produced by a heavily processed down-tuned and palm-muted power chord typically played on a 7- or 8-string guitar: "djent–djent" not "chugga–chugga."

Djent Recipe

1. Tune a 7-string guitar down one half step and then tune the 7th string down another whole step. Here's the tuning: 7(A♭), 6(E♭), 5(A♭), 4(D♭), 3(G♭), 2(B♭), 1(E♭). This is called drop A♭ tuning.

2. Now, play this power chord with some quick staccato jabs.

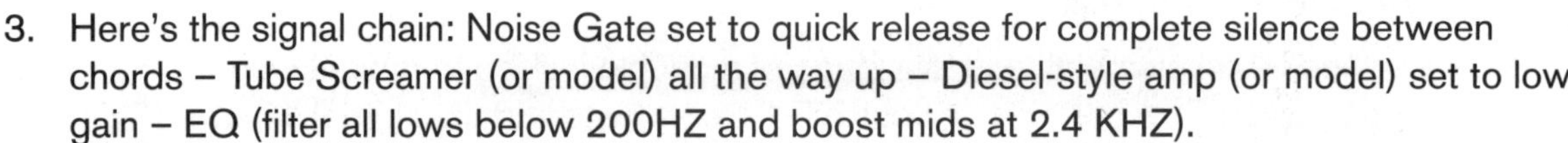

3. Here's the signal chain: Noise Gate set to quick release for complete silence between chords – Tube Screamer (or model) all the way up – Diesel-style amp (or model) set to low gain – EQ (filter all lows below 200HZ and boost mids at 2.4 KHZ).

We got this sound with a Fractal Axe-FX II, which is used by many djent artists, including Misha Mansoor of Periphery.

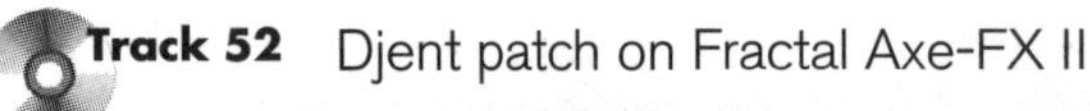

Track 52   Djent patch on Fractal Axe-FX II

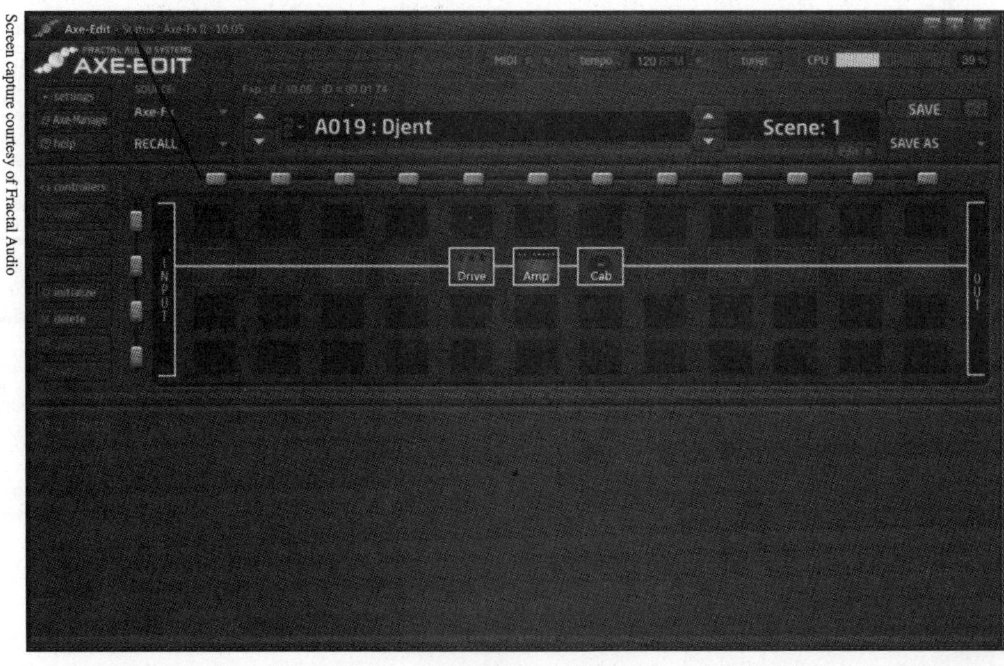

Screen capture courtesy of Fractal Audio

Over the Top Madness

Sometimes, the urge to overuse or "abuse" guitar effects can be so overwhelming that we just give in and go for it! This has spawned an entire movement called "noise guitar," not to mention moments of genius like Adrian Belew's elephant sounds in King Crimson's song "Elephant Talk" or David Gilmour's seagull sounds on "Echoes." Tom Morello's turntable and flute imitations come to mind as do The Edge's echo extravaganzas. Check out Tracks 53 and 54 for a couple of bizarre patches that render the guitar virtually unrecognizable. Sonic experimentation is fun!

Track 53 Fractal Stratosphere patch

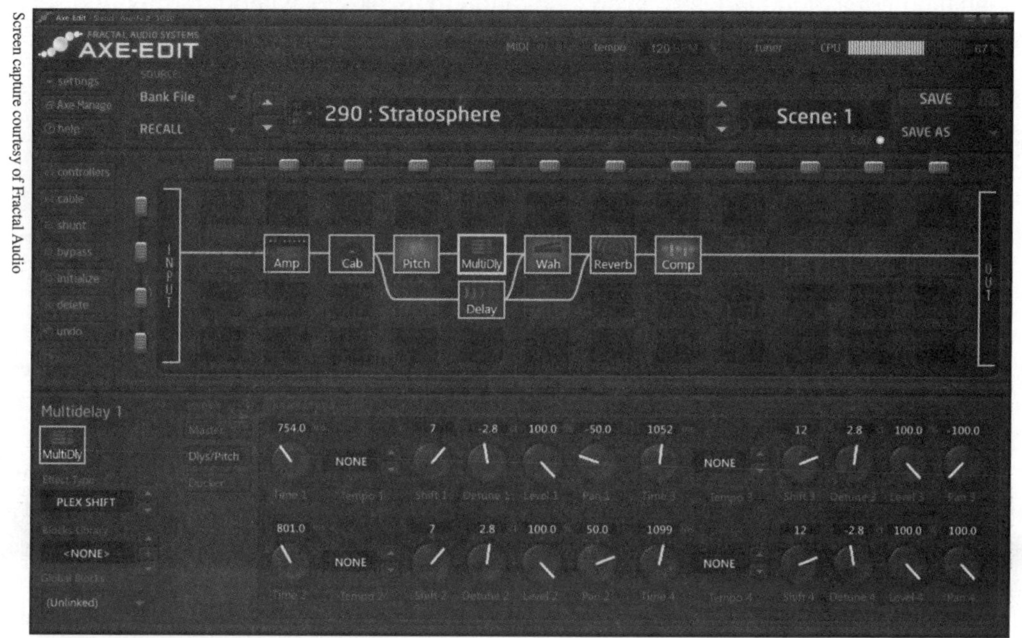

Track 54 Fractal Arpeggiating Synth patch

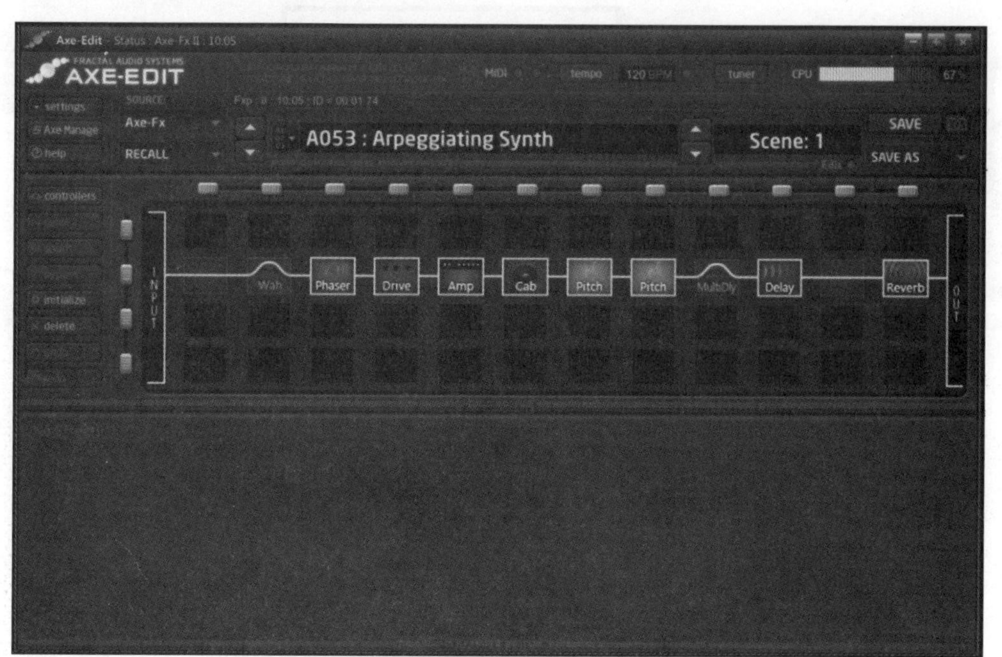

SETUPS OF LEGENDARY PLAYERS

Now, let's look at how to achieve the signature tones of some of the greatest players ever to plug a guitar into an amp.

The Eddie Van Halen Sound

Eddie Van Halen is one of those rare musicians whose innovations in technique and tone have played a key role in the evolution of the electric guitar. His popularization of the two-handed tapping technique spawned hordes of imitators as did his famous signature "brown" sound. Van Halen's constant output of guitar-driven hits, despite personnel changes in his band and the ever-shifting tides of the industry, is an inspiration to us all. So, without further ado, let's explore his signature sound—the "brown" sound.

The "brown" sound was a miraculous fluke, resulting from an odd combination of gear and lots of inspired tinkering. It can be heard on the early Van Halen albums. This stellar crunch was characterized by screaming highs that weren't harsh and a big warm bottom with just the right amount of midrange. Its most elusive quality was its elasticity, or sponginess, which gave the sound its unique feel. People have been trying for years, but no one can recreate the sound perfectly. It would seem that not even Van Halen himself can do it!

The ingredients of the mysterious "brown" sound were as follows: Van Halen's home made "Frankenstein" guitar was used, which featured an ash body, maple neck, and a single wax dipped Gibson PAF pickup in the bridge position. This Strat-style axe was equipped with a Floyd Rose locking tremolo and was strung with .009-.042 strings. The amp he used was a '66 or '67 Marshall 100-watt Super Lead head and 4x12 cabinet. A variac (variable transformer) was used to vary the power to the amp. The variac was adjusted so that the amp received less voltage than it really needed. This dangerous procedure resulted in the incredible elasticity of the sound but is also rumored to have ruined the amp. Don't try this at home! He also used an MXR Phase 90 pedal and an Echoplex. Listen to "Eruption" as recorded on *Van Halen* for a taste of the "brown" sound.

Track 55

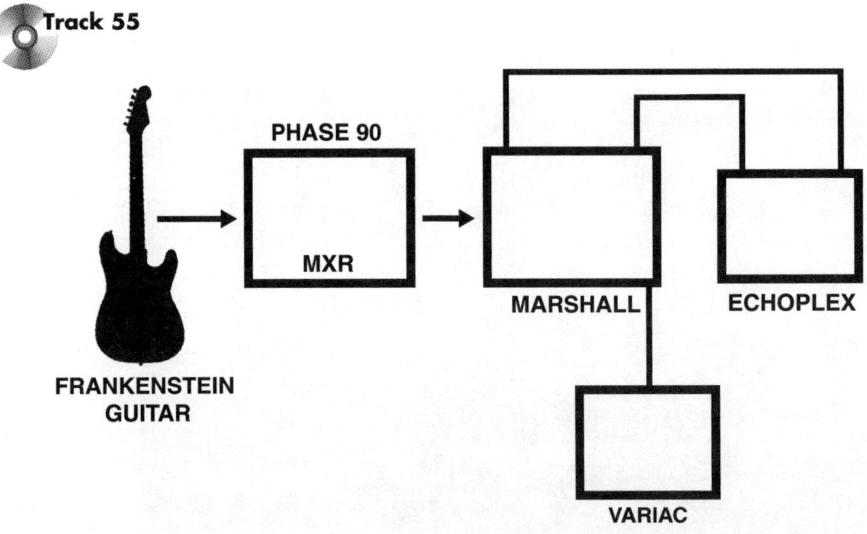

Below are a couple of ways to get close to the "brown" sound using gear that is readily available.

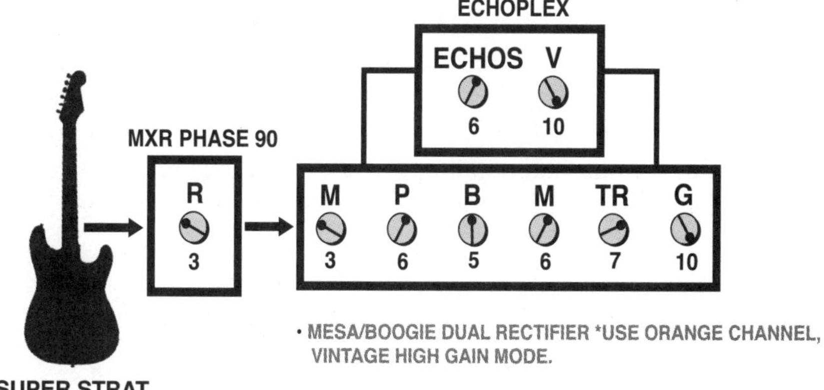

Tip: Switching to the tube rectifier of the Mesa/Boogie amp has an effect similar to the variac and produces a spongy sound. Also set the bold/spongy switch to spongy.

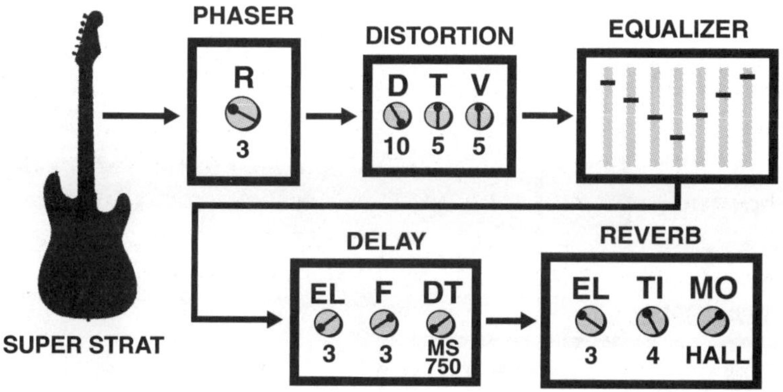

The Peavey Wolfgang Guitar

This guitar is made to Eddie's specs and named after his son. It features a basswood body with figured maple top, bolt-on bird's eye maple neck, and 22-fret fingerboard. The two humbuckers are custom made for low noise and high output. Controls include volume, tone, and a three-way selector. The bridge is a Floyd Rose double-locking tremolo with a *D-tuner* (a device that allows you to quickly drop the low-E string to D). This guitar is available in a variety of models.

Key to Abbreviations

B .... Bass	G .... Gain	R ...... Rate
DT .... Delay Time	M .... Midrange	TI ..... Time
D....... Distortion	MS ..... Milliseconds	TR.... Treble
EL ..... Effect Level	MO .... Mode	T ...... Tone
F........ Feedback	P .... Presence	V ...... Volume

The Jimi Hendrix Sound

Jimi Hendrix's legacy left us with enough groovy guitar lore to keep thousands of fingers twiddling for decades. But let's not forget the fact that he contributed a whole lot more than just cool songs and riffs to the guitarist's vocabulary. The thunder of his Strat, pumped through a chain of Marshall amps, was the war cry of the psychedelic era and has come to define rock and roll guitar tone. His studio experimentation yielded a rich palette of textures, ranging from backwards guitar to echo to sounds that pinged around the stereo field so much that they made the listener's head spin. Cranking *Electric Ladyland* in headphones is a must for any serious student of guitar tone or recording science.

Hendrix was left-handed and played mostly Stratocasters. He turned his axes upside down and reversed the strings so they would be more comfortable to play. Jimi didn't always use the same strings but he often chose light-gauge strings by Ernie Ball or Fender. Marshall 100-watt Super Lead heads and Marshall 4x12 cabinets were his amps of choice. The pedals he used live included a Vox wah, Roger Mayer Octavia, Arbitar Fuzz Face, and a Univox Univibe.

The diagram below shows the classic Hendrix setup.

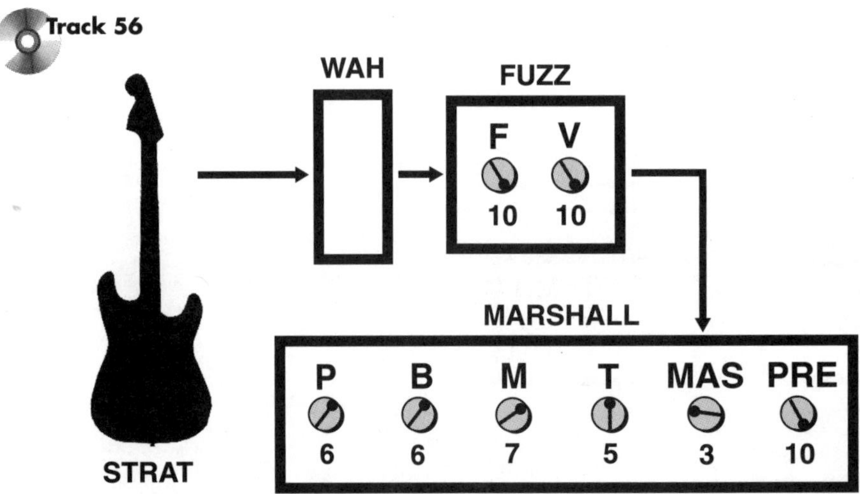

Key to Abbreviations

B ..... Bass	MAS.... Master	TI.... Time
D..... Distortion	M .... Midrange	T ..... Tone
EL ... Effect Level	MO ..... Mode	V ..... Volume
F...... Fuzz	P .... Presence	TI.... Delay Time
L...... Level	PRE .... Presonance	

For another take on Jimi's sound, tune down to E♭ and try these settings.

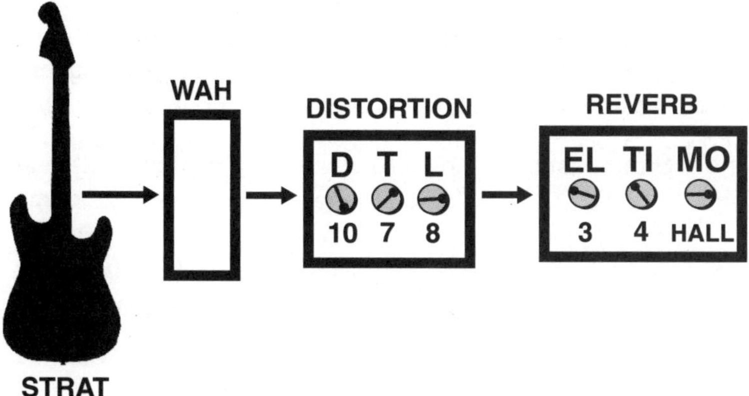

Fender's Jimi Hendrix Tribute Stratocaster

This guitar is a replica of the Strat Jimi used at Woodstock in 1969. It features an alder body, a maple neck, and a 21-fret maple fingerboard. This cool axe sports a large headstock with a psychedelic backwards Fender logo on it. The three single-coil pickups are vintage 1969 Alnicos* and are selected with a three-way switch. The vintage whammy bar hangs from the top of the bridge rather than its standard position at the bottom. Dig?

* The word "alnico" is an acronym consisting of the first two letters of the words "aluminum," "nickel," and "cobalt." The high-quality magnets in Alnico pickups contain these three elements.

The Tom Morello Sound

Since the 1990s, Tom Morello has been blowing audiences away with his slammin' riffs and groundbreaking tones for Rage Against the Machine and Audioslave. Sometimes, his guitar sounded like a scratching turntable; sometimes, he used stuttering kill-switch grooves with a lot of phase shifter; and sometimes, his guitar even sounded like a flute. He also used the Digitech Whammy Pedal to blast his shredding leads an octave higher than would be normally possible.

Morello mainly plays a modified Fender Stratocaster through a Marshall JCM 800 50-watt head and Peavey 4x12 cab. The modifications to his Strat include an Ibanez Edge Floyd Rose trem, a toggle-style kill switch (which he toggled back and forth to create his *stutter effect*), and a Seymour Duncan Hot Rails humbucker in the bridge position. He uses GHS .010–.046 gauge strings and often tunes to drop D. His modest pedalboard, which contains nothing terribly expensive or unusual, is diagrammed below.

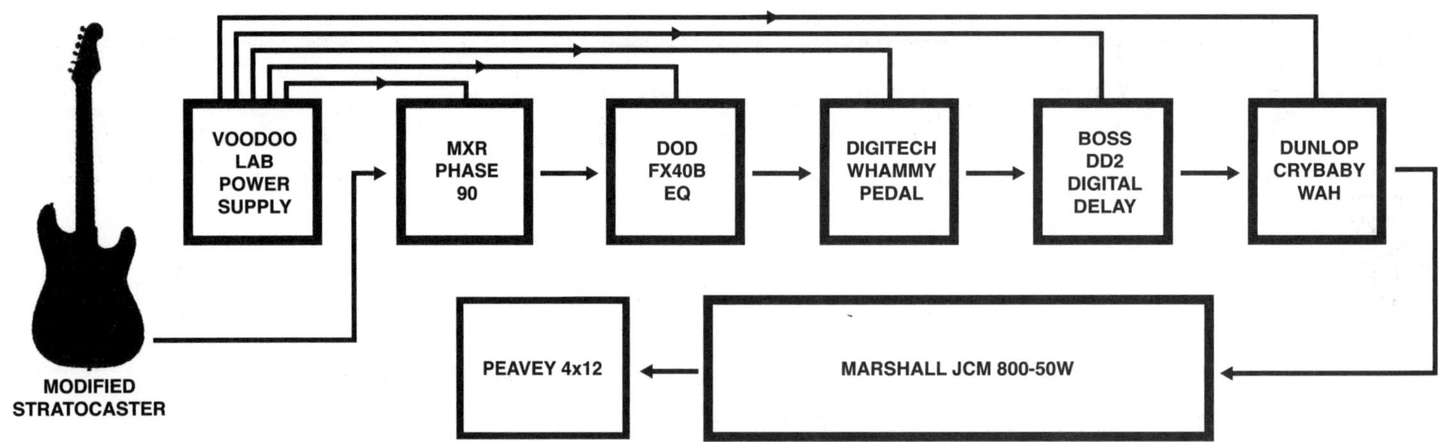

For Track 57, we've chosen a kill switch phaser/harmonizer riff with settings similar to Morello's on "Know Your Enemy." It requires the use of a guitar with Gibson Les Paul–type electronics, or any guitar with a kill switch. Set the harmonizer to one parallel 5th above the original note at about 30 percent volume. But before we get to the track, let's look a little closer at the stutter effect.

The Stutter Effect

This is how you get Tom Morello's stutter effect with a Gibson-style guitar: Set the tone and volume of the neck pickup all the way off and leave the tone and volume of the bridge pickup all the way up. Then the pickup selector switch acts as a kill switch. Push the switch downward to activate the pickup whenever you hammer-on to a note with the left hand.

To get the stutter effect with a kill switch–equipped guitar, push the switch to activate the guitar whenever you hammer-on to a note with the left hand.

Following are the settings we used to get the tone on Track 57.

Track 57

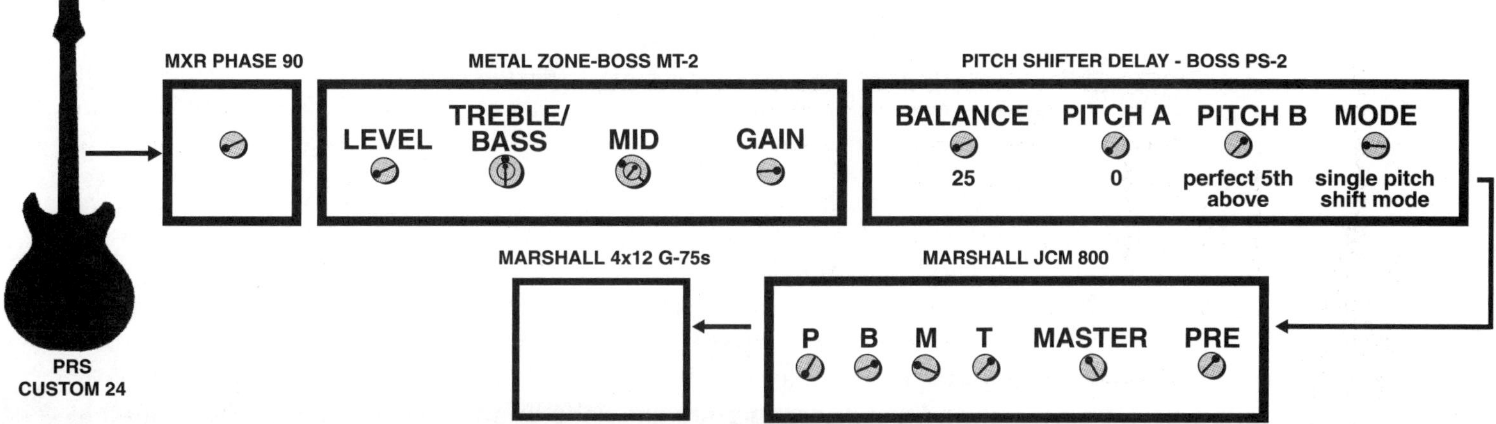

Fun Fact: *Tom Morello is a former student of Michael Angelo Batio.*

The Michael Angelo Batio Sound

Everyone's favorite shredder, Michael Angelo Batio, has distinguished himself as among the very fastest guitarists in the world. His extensive catalog of instrumental CDs and instructional products highlights his precision, consistency, and endurance at lightning tempos. During his decades of international touring, Batio has earned much respect and was voted "Fastest Guitarist in the World" by the readers of Guitar World Magazine in 2011. MAB's ambidextrous approach to playing his patented double guitar, which is on display in The Rock and Roll Hall of Fame, and his flamboyant "over-under" fingering technique have put him in a league of his own.

Angelo's tone is fairly simple, with the magic being mostly in his fingers. His typical setup includes two Marshall half stacks, two T-Rex MAB signature overdrive pedals, and two T-Rex Replica delays wired into the effects loops of the amps. (He has recently switched from Marshall tube amps to Dean Dime D100 120-watt solid-state amps.) Each neck of the double guitar goes into its own half stack with identical settings and effects. If he's playing a single guitar, it's usually his Dean Armor Flame signature model plugged into one Dime D100 amp with the same pedals. The Armor Flame comes stock with a Floyd Rose trem, 24 frets, a five-way blade switch, and three EMG active pickups. Angelo uses red Dunlop Jazz III picks and .009–.042 gauge strings. His double guitars are equipped with special patented MAB string dampers to enable clearly articulated playing.

He sets the amp heads for mid-gain, so that rolling off the guitar's volume knob produces a clean tone and the amp reverb is completely off. The overdrive pedal has the gain and drive set full up and the tone rolled slightly back for a warm sound. The delay is set to 320 milliseconds with minimal feedback, so that the third repeat is virtually inaudible. This subtle echo doesn't muddy up his sound. Michael is able to get quite a few tonal variations by switching his pickups and rolling off his volume for various clean and semi-clean sounds. Most of his shredding is done on the neck position pickup with the overdrive on for a warm sound.

Below is a setup used by Batio for many years. He switched from Marshall amps to Dean Dime D100 amps in 2010.

Track 58

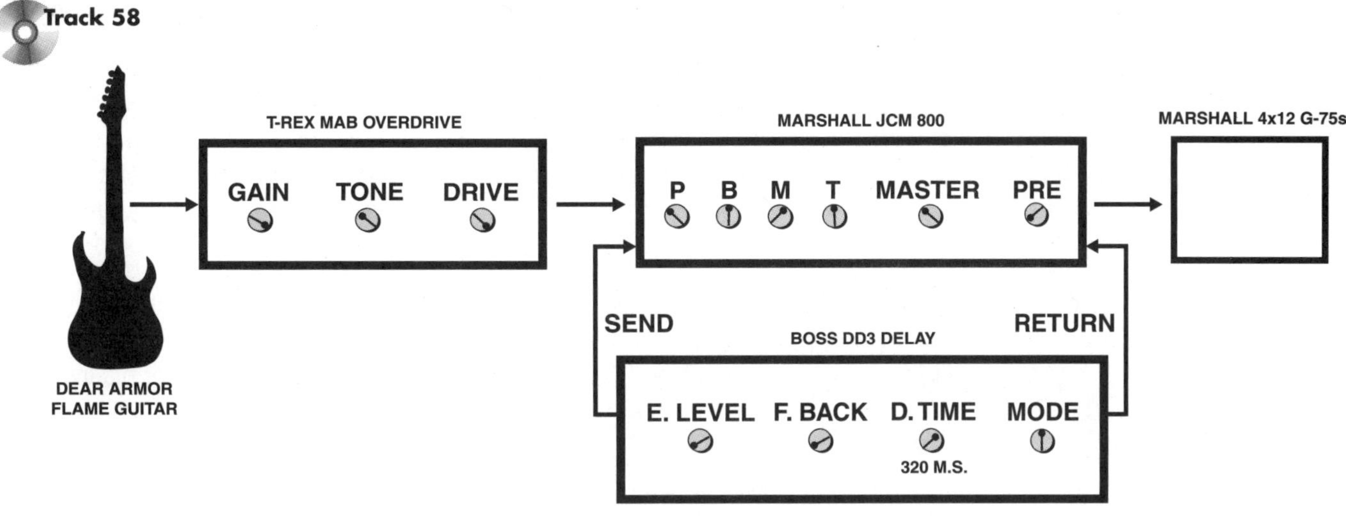

And here is his double guitar setup:

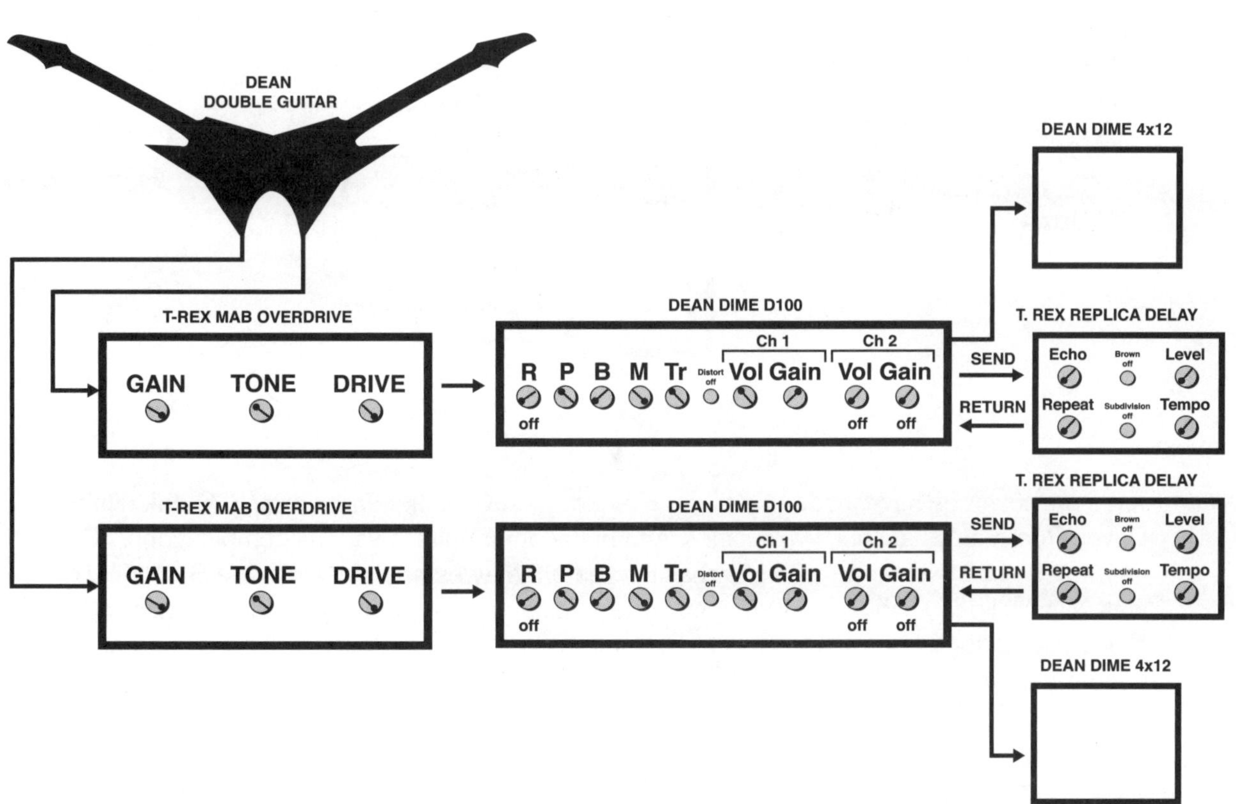

Key to Abbreviations

B ....Bass	P .... Presence
MAS...Master	REV ... Reverb
M ....Midrange	TR ..... Treble

The Joe Satriani Sound

Joe Satriani has been the champion of extreme instrumental guitar playing for over a decade now. Without compromising his vision, he has miraculously maintained solid success in this difficult market, never bowing to trends.

Satriani's incredible signature tone is a big part of his exhilarating musical persona. His fat, sustaining sound, with a slight vocal inflection on the attack of each note, is the product of lots of gear and much tweaking. His signature sound came into full bloom around the *Surfing with the Alien* period. Though Joe always sounds like himself, his tone has seen a lot of changes from song to song and album to album.

"Satch" uses D'Addario .09–.042 strings. He consistently uses Ibanez JS (Joe Satriani) model guitars and Marshall amps and cabinets, but the rest of his gear remains in a state of flux. He has been downsizing his rig for a number of years now. Below is a block diagram of his live/ studio rig during the G-3 tour (circa 1997).

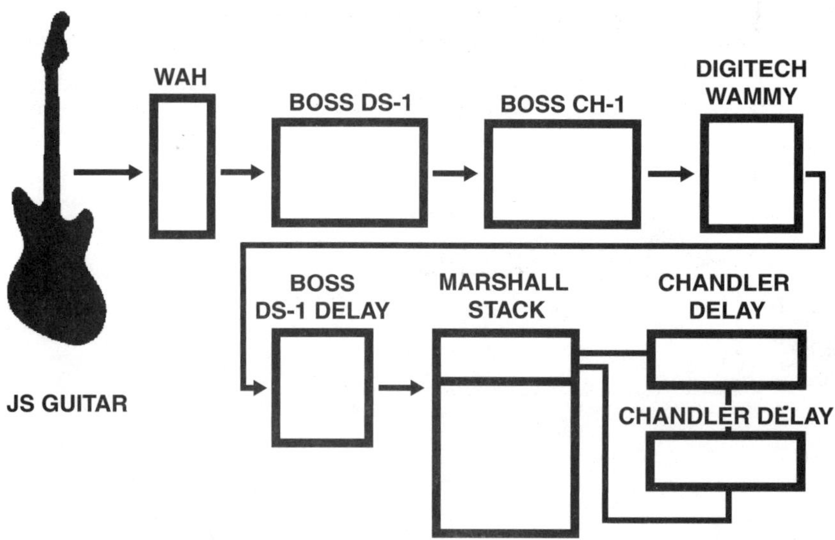

Joe's previous rigs have made use of the Eventide H3000 Ultra-Harmonizer, Chandler Tube Driver, Rockman Sustainer, Wells amps, and many other units in various combinations. (Most recently, he has teamed up with Marshall to create the awesome signature Joe Satriani 100-watt Marshall head, which is a JVM with added noise gates and special channel voicings.) Since putting together such a rig would be impossible for most of us, we'll be looking at a more user-friendly alternative to copy his sound.

The Rocktron Chameleon

The Chameleon was a high-quality single rack space multi-effects device. The original units had a pre-set called "Satriani." Whoever programmed that preset was right on the money because it sounds a lot like Satch!

If you were to look at the effects chain within the Chameleon as a series of separate stomp boxes, it would look like the diagram below. If you don't happen to own a Chameleon but you do have pedals, try these settings for a great Satch tone!

Track 59

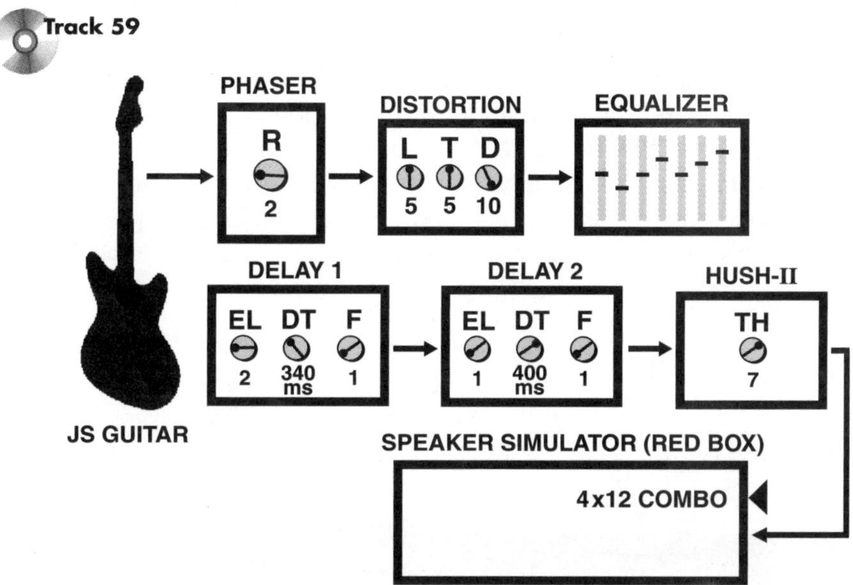

The Ibanez JS Model Guitars

The JS guitar features a 22-fret rosewood fingerboard and a lightweight basswood body. The bridge is the Ibanez Edge tremolo with a locking nut. Two high-output DiMarzio pickups are used, the FRED in the bridge position and the PAF Pro in the neck position. The guitar features a three-way pickup selector switch. The JS-6 model is not tremolo-equipped and features a mahogany body. These guitars are very comfortable to play and sound great, especially if you want to sound like Joe Satriani!

Key to Abbreviations

DT ..... Delay Time	F ..... Feedback	TH ..... Threshold
D .... Distortion	L ..... Level	T .... Tone
EL ...... Effect Level	R .... Rate	

The Randy Rhoads Sound

Randy Rhoads' blazing guitar work during his two-album stint with Ozzy Osbourne in the early 1980s marked an important step in the evolution of classically influenced rock guitar. His work continued where the likes of Ritchie Blackmore left off and gave newer players like Yngwie Malmsteen a solid platform to jump off from.

Randy Rhoads' blistering riffs and tones on those Ozzy Osbourne albums certainly rank among the greatest metal recordings of all time. His main axe at that time was a 1964 cream Les Paul strung with GHS .010–.046 strings. Randy also enjoyed playing flying Vs and had a Kahler-equipped signature model built by Jackson. He was a believer in solid-state technology, using Peavey amps and MXR pedals for his raw sound. His MXR pedals included the Distortion Plus, EQ, Flanger, and Chorus. He also had a Cry Baby wah and a Korg echo.

Randy used one very unconventional studio trick to get his fat crunch. He double- or triple-tracked many of his parts. This means he played two or three virtually identical parts on separate tracks. These tracks were then blended for a fatter sound. The small differences in timing and inflection from track to track created a natural chorusing effect that was very musical. Double- and triple-tracking has traditionally been more popular among horn players and vocalists than guitarists. Randy broke away from the pack by using this offbeat technique to fatten his sound.

The following setup will get you the Randy Rhoads sound:

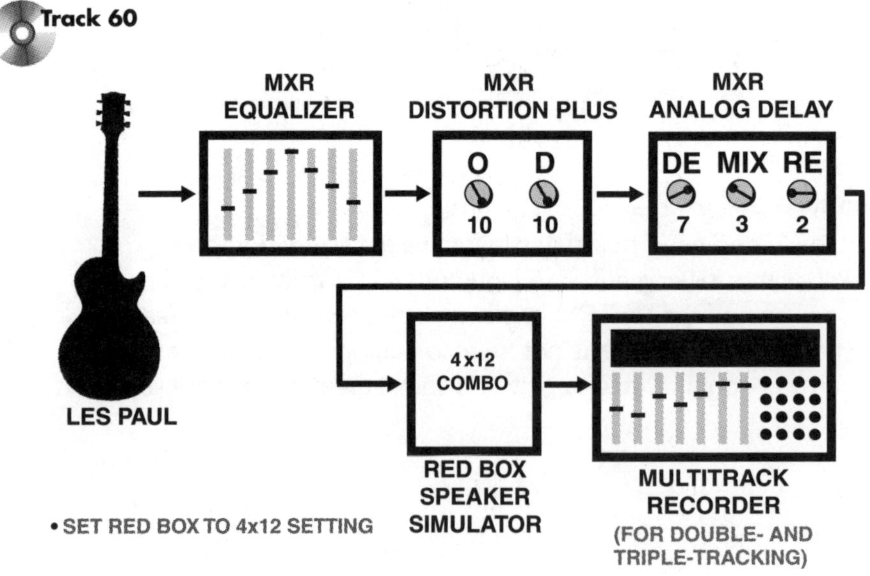

Electronic Double-Tracking

Double-tracking can be electronically produced by using a delay. Set the delay time for a quick echo so that the echo is almost simultaneous with the original sound. Try between 5 and 50 milliseconds. The more milliseconds, the "looser" the double will sound. Set the feedback control to one repeat and the mix control so that the volume of the wet signal is slightly below that of the dry one. These settings create a clone of the source that is slightly displaced in time and sounds like another player doubling the part. Electronic double-tracking doesn't create the natural chorusing effect of the real thing, but it fattens up a live tone considerably. Try the settings below.

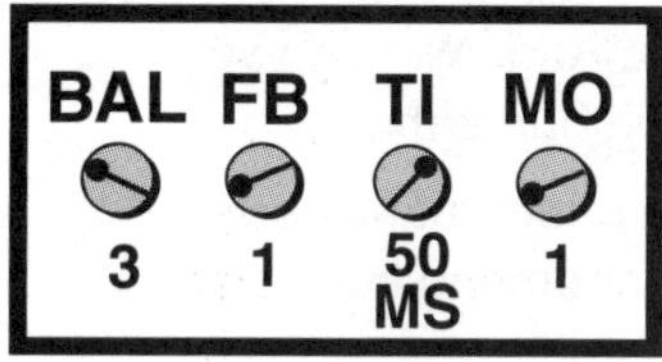

The Randy Rhoads Tribute Model Guitar

Jackson Guitars made only 200 Randy Rhoads Tribute Model guitars. This limited run of cool axes was designed to faithfully copy Randy's own flying V. The guitar is an offset V with pinstripes and rectangular neck inlays. It features a maple neck and body with a 22-fret ebony fingerboard fitted with small frets. Seymour Duncan high-output humbucking pickups were used in the neck position (jazz-style) and in the bridge position (distortion style). The vintage-style tremolo is a heavy duty brass unit made by Kahler. Jackson has improved the design of the newer mass-produced Rhoads Model guitars by streamlining the body and using different pickups and hardware.

Key to Abbreviations

BAL....Balance	MS ......Milliseconds	O.....Output
DE .....Delay	MIX....Mix	RE...Regeneration
D........Distortion	MO .....Mode	TI....Time
FB ......Feedback		

Finally, let's return to where it all started—just plugging a great-sounding guitar into a great amp.

The Charlie Christian Sound

Jazz guitarist Charlie Christian was born in Texas in 1916. He was one of the first amplified electric guitarists to bring the guitar out of the background and into the spotlight as a credible melodic instrument in the ensemble setting. His pioneering work with The Benny Goodman Orchestra from 1939 to 1941 had him soloing in turn with many instruments that were naturally much louder than an acoustic guitar. Without his Gibson ES-150 and combo amp, it would have been impossible for him to be heard. These days, it's commonplace to see an electric guitar alongside horns, drums, and pianos. Thanks, Charlie! Where would we be without you?

Christian's tone was pure, sweet, and fat—the way jazz is supposed to sound. For Track 61, we used a Gibson ES-120 strung with 12-gauge D'Addarios and plugged into a vintage Premier 1x10 tube combo. A touch of reverb and delay were added in the mix. And swinging some diminished 7th arpeggios with chromatic passing tones mixed in didn't hurt either!

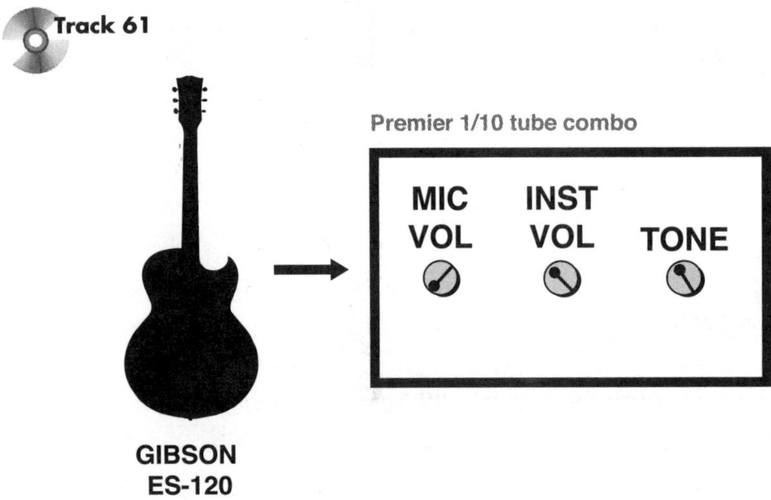

Next, we plugged the same guitar into a 1940s Fender Deluxe. Note the sonic difference—less air, more beef!

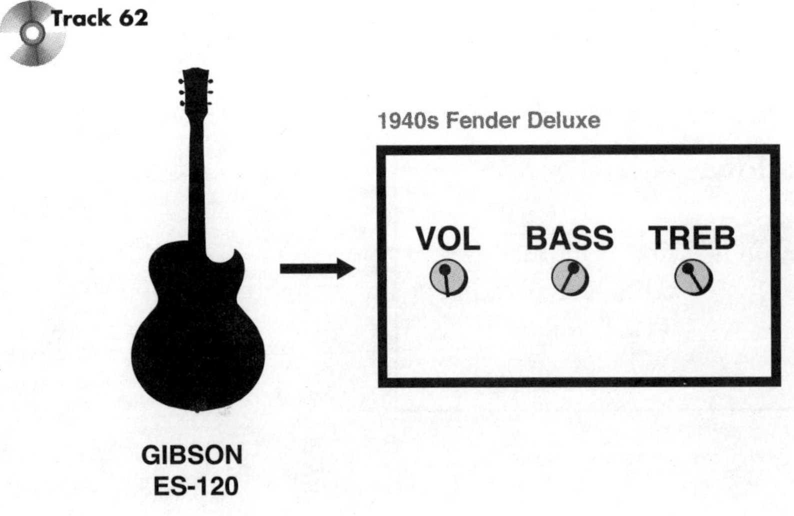

Charlie Christian (1916–1942).

CONCLUSION

Congratulations! You made it through *The Serious Guitarist: Essential Book of Gear*. This huge topic was a blast to research, and I hope you enjoyed reading about it as much as I enjoyed writing about it. You have gained lots of practical knowledge, like how to avoid burning up your amp when hooking up the speakers, how to eliminate the noise in your rig, and how to adjust a truss rod, among other things. It might also be safe to assume that there are a few more items on your gear wish list after staring at so many pictures throughout this book.

Even though *The Serious Guitarist: Essential Book of Gear* is a whopping 128 pages long, I still agonize over what made the cut and what didn't. There's just too much great gear out there to list and discuss it all. With that said, you now have a pretty good idea of the big picture, and I hope it serves you well. Good luck, and may you achieve the perfect tone!

Additional Reading

Bacon, Tony • *The History of the American Guitar* • Outline Press LTD, 2001

Bacon, Tony • *Electric Guitars: The Illustrated Encyclopedia* • Thunder Bay Press, 2000

Davis/Jones • *Sound Reinforcement Handbook* • Yamaha, 1989

Kitts, Jeff • *The Complete History of Guitar World: 30 Years of Music, Magic, and Six String Mayhem* • Backbeat Books, 2010

Molenda, Michael • *The Guitar Player Book* • Backbeat, 2007

Pittman, Aspen • *The Tube Amp Book (4.1th Edition)* • Groove Tubes, 1995

Thompson, Art • *The Stompbox: A History of Guitar Fuzzes, Flangers, Phasers, Echoes and Wahs* • Miller Freeman, 1997